Scandinavian Designs
in Red and White

Craft and Sew 55 Beautiful Projects for the Home

Nadja Knab-Leers • Heike Roland • Stefanie Thomas

Scandinavian Designs
in Red and White

Craft and Sew 55 Beautiful Projects for the Home

Contents

This year, why not add some colourful red-and-white accents to your garden,
patio or conservatory? Whether you want to make decorations,
such as lanterns and pennants, or practical items, such as a gardening apron,
red and white will always be eye-catching colours in a green garden.

Grey day? Not anymore! These practical little helpers will cheer up
your daily chores. Not only do aprons and towels, etc. make everyday
living easier, but they can also make it nicer.

Are you looking for some decorative ideas to freshen up your home? Then take a
look at this section. Here you will find red-and-white decorations including candle
arrangements, picture frames and fun dolls to brighten every room.

Give a little happiness! At the next opportunity, make your dearest
friends, family and relatives a present in red and white.
Even a greetings card will bring cheer in this lively colour combination.

This section contains the basic techniques needed for the projects, such as
sewing, using paper napkins for découpage or working with wood, and you
will find some useful tips and tricks here too. You will also find the patterns
required for making some of the items in this book.

Introduction

Red and white is a fresh and fashionable colour combination. The lively contrast of clear white and bright red is an expression of pure joy and happiness. The colours of strawberries and cream and bright toadstools also make us think of Scandinavia, not least because of the red wooden houses with their gleaming white window frames and doors. These two colours, and their delicate intermediate shades of pink, have provided us with the inspiration for this book.

We have created pretty decorations and practical items for indoors and out so that you can bring the joy and liveliness of red and white into your daily life. Cosy cushions and gorgeous lanterns will help you unwind in the garden, and there is a pretty and practical gardening apron and kneeling pad to ensure that you enjoy your gardening too. In the home, red and white can form charming accents with little dolls, kitchen utensils and beautiful decorations, such as vases or picture frames. We also have some gift ideas for spreading a little red and white happiness!

We think you will find our enthusiasm for red and white somewhat infectious. We wish you lots of fun making these items.

In the Garden

In warm weather, we can extend our living space outside into a garden or patio, to enjoy the sunshine and to entertain friends and family. Bring cheer to a festive *al fresco* meal with a red-and-white table set; work outdoors in style and comfort with our garden accessories and, after all that effort, relax back into our pretty cushions with a long, cool drink and, as the sun sets, light the lanterns to make the evening last longer.

Picnic with Panache

Menu

Patchwork tablecloth

• 2m (2¼ yd) of white fabric with small red flowers • 50cm (½ yd) of red fabric with white spots • 50cm (½ yd) of gingham fabric • 1m (1yd) of cotton fabric decorated with vegetables • 7m (7¾ yd) red rickrack braid, 1cm (⅜in) wide • 1m (1yd) of fusible web, such as Bondaweb • Refer to the diagram on page 84. Seam allowances are 1cm (⅜in).

For the centre part of the tablecloth, cut out 28 squares measuring 20 × 20cm (8 × 8in): 10 in floral fabric, 8 in spotted fabric and 10 in gingham fabric. You will also need 2 strips measuring 140 × 35cm (55 × 13¾in) and 2 strips measuring 150 × 35cm (59 × 13¾in) for the outer frame, cut from the larger piece of fabric.

❈

Referring to the diagram on page 84, first join the squares into 4 long strips, each containing 7 squares. Neaten all the seam edges and iron the seam allowances, alternating towards the inside or the outside. Now sew all four long strips together, with right sides facing, as in the diagram, making sure that the squares line up exactly with one another and that the seam allowances are staggered. Neaten all the seams together as far as the outside edges and iron the seam allowances towards the inside or the outside, alternating.

❈

To make the outer frame, first sew the long strips of fabric to the long edges of the patchwork, then the two shorter strips to the short edges of the patchwork. Neaten the edges together and iron flat. Now neaten the outside edges of the fabric frame: press a small seam allowance to the wrong side and sew rickrack braid on to the right side, so that the curves overlap the edge a little.

❈

Cut out the fusible web roughly to the size of the each vegetable motif and use it to fuse a motif to the centre of each floral fabric square (see page 82).

Lanterns

- 30cm (12in) of spotted fabric • 18cm (7in) of gingham fabric • 17cm (6¾in) of floral fabric • 30cm (12in) of cotton fabric decorated with vegetables • 5mm (¼in) and 1.5cm (⅝in) wide gingham ribbon and 1.5cm (½in) wide spotted satin ribbon • White cardboard containers, 9.5cm (3¾in) and 13cm (5in) in diameter • Iron-on fabric stiffener • Remnant of fusible web, such as Bondaweb • Textile adhesive • White eyelets, about 4mm (³⁄₁₆in) in diameter, plus an eyelet punch

Use the 13cm (5in) diameter container lid for the base of the large lantern. For the base of one small lantern, use the 9.5cm diameter (3¾in) lid; use the lower part of the small container for the other small lantern.

Cut the following rectangles from fabric and iron-on fabric stiffener: 23 × 45cm (9 × 18in) for the spotted lantern, 18 × 35cm (7 × 14in) for the checked lantern and 16 × 32cm (6¼ × 12½in) for the floral lantern. Fix the stiffener to the fabric following the manufacturer's instructions. These are your covers.

Before the covers are fixed to the lid bases, fix two eyelets to one edge to hold the ribbon handle, using the photograph as a guide. Use the fusible web to bond a vegetable motif on to the centre of each cover (see page 82). Attach the lantern cover with textile adhesive to the corresponding lid/container, overlapping the edges and gluing them down. Glue ribbon on to the top and bottom edges of the covers. To hang the lanterns, thread more ribbon through the eyelets and knot the ends inside.

Napkins

- 45cm (17¾in) square of red-and-white floral fabric for each napkin • 30cm (12in) of cotton fabric decorated with vegetables • 2m (2¼yd) of red rickrack braid, 1cm (⅝in) wide • 1m (1yd) of red satin ribbon with white spots, 1.5cm (⅝in) wide • Wadding or toy stuffing • 18 green rocaille beads

Neaten the outside edges of each fabric square. Iron the neatened edges to the wrong side and sew the rickrack braid all around on the reverse side, so that the curves are visible from the right side.

For the pendant, roughly cut out the desired vegetable motif, pin right sides together on a remnant of floral fabric and sew together along the edges, leaving 2cm (¾in) open for turning out. Turn out the motif, iron flat, fill with wadding and sew up the opening by hand using mattress stitch. Thread the beads on to strong thread and attach them to the top of the motif to make a hanging loop. Now the pendant can be hung from a ribbon and tied around the folded napkin.

Menu cards

- 21 × 25cm (8 ¼ × 10in) rectangle of red-and-white card
- Copier paper • Remnant of fusible web, such as Bondaweb
- Remnants of cotton fabric decorated with vegetables • Red fabric marker pen

Fold the card in half lengthways. Cut the copier paper 2–3mm (⅛in) smaller all round for an insert and fold. Iron the motif on to the card using fusible web, following the instructions on page 82, and write on it using the red marker pen. Write the menu details on the insert and place it inside the card.

Watering-can vase

- Mini metal watering can, about 21 × 10cm (8 ¼ × 4in)
- 70cm (27 ½ in) of spotted red-and-white satin ribbon, 1.5cm (⅝ in) wide • Vegetable cut-out

Tie the ribbon around the watering can in a bow. Glue the vegetable cut-out on to the front of the can in the centre. For this table decoration, the little watering can was filled with parsley.

The Stylish Gardener

Gardener's apron

• 60cm (24in) of red fabric with white spots • 30cm (12in) of white fabric with a red floral motif
• 20cm (8in) of gingham fabric • remnant of red fabric with large white spots for the toadstool motif
• 30cm (12in) of fusible wadding, 1.5m (60in) wide • 1m (1yd) of fusible interfacing • 15cm (6in) of
fusible web, such as Bondaweb • 1.1m (1 ¼ yd) of red checked cotton bias binding, 2cm (¾ in) wide
• 20cm (8in) of red-and-white Vichy check ribbon, 5mm (¼ in) wide • 2 red wooden clothes pegs (or
paint two plain clothes pegs red) • Mini toadstool embellishments to adorn the pegs, if available • Refer
to the pattern on page 84 and the diagram on page 94. Seam allowances are 1cm (⅜ in).

Cut two 55 × 28cm (22 × 11in) pieces of red spotted fabric and a piece of wadding the same size. Place the fabric rectangles wrong sides together, with the wadding in between, and iron to fuse the layers. For the pockets, cut one 71 × 24cm (28 × 9½in) rectangle of both the red spotted fabric and the floral fabric and two 71 × 24cm (28 × 9½in) rectangles of interfacing. Fuse the interfacing to the wrong side of each pocket fabric. For the waistband tape, cut a 230 × 8cm (90½ × 3in) strip of gingham fabric, joining pieces as necessary to make up the length. Cut a matching length of interfacing and fuse it to the wrong side of the gingham strip. Fuse stabiliser to the wrong side of some spotted and checked fabric scraps and cut out the toadstools from page 84 (see page 82 for more details).

Pin together both pieces of fabric for the pockets along one long edge, right sides together. Sew together, taking a 1cm (⅜in) seam allowance and leaving a gap to turn through. Turn out, iron the seam flat and topstitch following the width of the sewing-machine foot. Iron pleats into the pocket piece according to the diagram (see page 94) and topstitch all the creases of the folds inside and out close to the edge, making sure that the floral fabric is on the outside when the apron is complete.

Place the pocket piece along one long edge of the wadded apron, round off the corners, pin both pieces together and topstitch close to the edge, making sure that you catch in the folds at the bottom of the pocket the same time. Now mark the centre of each fold along the length, pin on to wadded apron and sew down, separating the pockets. Attach the bias binding to the edge of the apron, leaving the top long edge free.

Turn a 1cm (⅜in) allowance under on both long edges of the waistband tape and press, then iron the strips in half lengthways. Finish both ends at an angle, stitching the angled edges together, close to the edge, right sides facing and turn out. Push the top long edge of the apron piece centred between the open edges of the tape and pin together with a 1cm (⅜in) overlap. Topstitch the tape close to the edge, catching in the apron at the same time.

Attach the fabric toadstools using fusible web, following the instructions on page 82. Tie gingham ribbon in a bow and sew by hand on to the large toadstool. Glue a mini toadstool and a bow made from gingham ribbon to the centre of each peg.

Kneeling pad

• 1.1m (1¼yd) of red vinyl fabric with white spots • 20cm (8in) square of white fabric with a red floral motif • Remnants of red-and-white spotted and gingham fabrics for the toadstools • 20cm (8in) square of fusible film, such as Lamifix • 20cm (8in) of fusible web, such as Bondaweb • Decorative-edge scissors • Wadding • Refer to the pattern on page 84.

Cut a 102 × 34cm (40 × 13½in) rectangle of vinyl fabric for the cover and a strip 40 × 7cm (16 × 2¾in) for the handle.

Iron the fusible web to the back of the scraps of fabric and cut out the toadstool appliqués given on page 84 (see page 82). Fuse these to the floral fabric square. Fix the Lamifix to the floral fabric, following the manufacturer's instructions, to give it a protective covering. Cut all around the edge with the decorative-edge scissors. Stitch the fabric close to the edges, centred on the kneeling-pad cover. To position the fabric accurately, fold the kneeling pad cover wrong sides together along the length.

Fold the fabric strip in half lengthways, right sides together, and stitch together along the long edges following the width of the sewing-machine foot. Turn the strip out and iron flat. Fold the kneeling-pad cover in half along the length, right sides together. Place the handle in between on one of the short edges with a 16cm (6¼in) gap, remembering that the main part of the handle needs to be between the two fabrics so that it is on the outside when the fabrics are turned right way out. Stitch up the open edges following the width of the sewing-machine foot, leaving a 10cm (4in) opening for turning. Turn the kneeling pad out, fill firmly with wadding and sew up the opening by hand using mattress stitch.

Gardening gloves

• White leather work gloves with hook-and-loop (Velcro) fastening • 20cm (8in) of red-and-white fabric with large dots • 40cm (16in) of red-and-white fabric with small dots • 60cm (24in) of fusible interfacing • 50cm (19 ½ in) of white rickrack braid, 1cm (⅜in) wide • Refer to pattern sheets A and B.

Transfer the patterns to the relevant fabric: piece A and C once for each glove on to the fabric with small dots, piece B once on to the fabric with large dots. Cut out the pieces. Cut out all the pieces once more from the interfacing and iron this on to the wrong side of the fabric.

❁

Sew pieces A and B together along the straight edge, right sides together, taking a 1cm (⅜in) seam allowance and placing rickrack braid in between, so that the curves are visible from the right side; press flat. Place this piece and piece C right sides together and stitch all around, following the width of the sewing machine foot, and leaving 10cm (4in) open for turning. Turn the cuff right side out and close the open edge by hand using mattress stitch.

❁

Separate the hook-and-loop fastening for securing the lower flap of the glove. Stitch the finished cuff to the glove close to the edge, catching in the closure strap on the upper flap (stitch on the edge). Stitch the separated hook-and-loop fastening for the closure to the corresponding lower flap on the cuff.

Watering can

• *Metal watering can* • *Durable acrylic paint in red and white, suitable for use on metal*
• *Masking tape* • *Refer to the pattern on page 84.*

Decorate the watering can in red and white acrylic paint, referring the photograph as a guide. When painting, it can be helpful to stick masking tape along the straight edges. The curved edges must be painted freehand. Make sure that you paint all the surfaces twice to give good coverage.

Trace the toadstools on page 84 and transfer them to the centre of the watering can. Paint the motifs using the acrylic paint.

Tip

Make a plant marker to match the watering can. First paint a wooden plant marker with white acrylic paint. Next apply two to three coats of chalkboard paint to the text area. You can then decorate the plant marker as shown in the photograph.

Flowerpots

- 3 unglazed flowerpots • Durable acrylic paint in red and white • Black permanent marker pen

Paint the pots with simple patterns as shown in the photograph. Start with the white areas, leaving the areas that are to be painted red blank. Apply two coats to get good coverage.

Next, paint the inside of the pots red along with the red areas on the outside. A second coat may well be needed here too. Use the marker pen to add decorative broken lines, like the stitches in patchwork.

Herb markers

- 20 × 30cm (8 × 12in) of plywood, roughly 4mm (³⁄₁₆in) thick • Durable acrylic paint in red and white • White permanent gel pen • Black permanent marker pen • Red-and-white gingham ribbon • 3 wooden skewers • Refer to the pattern on page 84.

Using the pattern on page 84, cut out a large heart and heart frame for each marker using a jigsaw; sand the edges smooth. Paint both pieces, using the photograph as your guide. Glue a heart frame on to each heart.

Decorate the plant markers with the gel pen and write on the signs with the black permanent marker pen. Attach one skewer to the back of each sign with strong glue, preferably hot glue. Tie the ribbon in a bow around the skewer.

Appliquéd cushion

- 52 × 32cm (20 ½ × 12 ½ in) rectangle of white cotton fabric (top front of the cushion) • 52 × 19cm (20 ½ × 7 ½ in) rectangle of pink floral cotton fabric (bottom front of the cushion) • 52cm (20 ½ in) square of dark red cotton fabric for the back • White cotton fabric and remnants of coloured cotton fabrics for the appliqué motifs (or use ready-made appliqué motifs) • 52cm (20 ½ in) of 1cm (⅜in) wide textile braid in light blue with pink flowers • 70cm (28in) of 1cm (⅜in) wide textile braid in pink with dark red flowers • 122cm (48in) of 1cm (⅜in) wide pink rickrack braid • 50cm (19 ½ in) white zip fastener • Refer to pattern sheet B. Seam allowances are 1cm (⅜in).

Cut two 32cm (12½in) pieces of pink rickrack braid and two 32cm (12½in) pieces of pink textile braid and stitch these on to each end edge of the white cotton fabric, placing the rickrack braid 2.5cm (1in) from the edge and the textile braid 1cm (⅜in) in from it. Sew the white cotton fabric to the floral cotton with right sides facing. Stitch the remaining rickrack braid on to the seam. Sew the light blue textile braid about 1.5cm (⅝in) away from the top edge of the white fabric.

Trace the appliqué motifs from pattern sheet B and fuse them to your chosen fabrics (see page 82). Fuse these to white cotton fabric then embroider the details. Cut around the shapes, leaving a small seam allowance. Turn the allowance under all round and stitch the appliqués on to the front of the cushion, using the photograph as a guide. Sew the zip fastener to the lower edge of the cushion between the two cushion pieces. Open the zip a little. Stitch both cushion pieces together, right sides facing and turn the cushion out through the zip opening.

Rose cushion

- Two 32 × 23cm (12 ½ × 9in) rectangles of rose-print cotton fabric • Two 32 × 11cm (12 ½ × 4 ½ in) rectangles of white cotton • 32cm (12 ½ in) of pink rickrack braid, 1cm (⅜in) wide • 32cm (12 ½ in) of white textile braid with a pink floral design, 1cm (⅜in) wide • 30cm (12in) white zip fastener

For the front of the cushion, sew one white fabric strip to the rose-print cotton along the matching edge, placing them right sides together with raw edges matching. Taking a 1cm (⅜in) seam allowance, topstitch the seam. Sew the textile braid 1.5cm (⅝in) above the seam (on the white fabric) and the rickrack braid 1cm (⅜in) above that.

Sew the zip fastener between the two remaining fabrics to make the back piece and open the zip a little way. Taking a 1cm (⅜in) seam allowance, sew both cushion pieces together, right sides facing, so that the same fabrics line up. Turn the cushion out through the opening for the zip fastening.

Lazy Days

Striped cushion

• 40cm (16in) of white cotton fabric • Cotton fabrics for the stripes — we used pink-and-red spotted fabric, pink fabric with diamond shapes, light blue floral fabric, pink-and-red floral fabric, light blue fabric with white spots and dark red fabric • 52cm (20 ½ in) of textile braid in light blue with pink flowers, 1cm (⅜in) wide • 52cm (20 ½ in) of pink rickrack braid, 1cm (⅜in) wide • 50cm (20in) white zip fastener

Cut strips from the fabric remnants in the following measurements: 5 × 15cm (2 × 6in) strip of pink-and-red spotted fabric (strip 2); 6 × 15cm (2¼ × 6in) strip of pink diamond fabric (strip 4) and 100 × 6cm (39½ × 2¼in) of the same fabric for the frill; 5 × 15cm (2 × 6in) strip of blue floral fabric (strip 6); 6 × 15cm (2¼ × 6in) strip of pink-and-red floral fabric (strip 8); 5 × 15cm (2 × 6in) strip of spotted blue fabric (strip 10), and one 5 × 15cm (2 × 6in) strip of dark red fabric (strip 12).

From the white fabric cut the following pieces: 52 × 37cm (20½ × 14½in) for the cushion back; 52 × 15cm (20½ × 6in) for the bottom front of the cushion; 15 × 24cm (20½ × 9½in) strip (strip 1); 6 × 15 cm (2¼ × 6in) strip (strip 3); two 5.5 × 15cm (2¼ × 6in) strips (strips 7 +11) and two 5 × 15cm (2 × 6in) strips (strips 5 + 9).

For the top panel of the cushion, join the strips in number order, referring to the photograph on page 19 and taking a 1cm (⅜in) seam allowance. Join the pieces with right sides facing.

Fold the frill in half lengthways with wrong sides together. Along the cut long raw edges work a line of running stitch through both layers within the seam allowance and pull the thread to gather the frill to fit the cushion (52cm/20½in). Sew the bottom front of the cushion to the top panel, catching the frill in between, with right sides together.

Stitch the textile braid 8cm (3in) above the bottom edge of the cushion and the rickrack braid 1cm (⅜in) below it. Sew the zip fastener to the bottom edge of the cushion between the front and back pieces. Open the zip a little way. Join the front to the back, right sides facing, and turn the cushion out through the zip opening.

To make the bunting, see overleaf.

Bunting

• 25cm (10in) each of three different cotton fabrics in red, white and pink combinations • 3m (3 ¼ yd) of pink bias binding, 2cm (¾in) wide • 50cm (½ yd) of pink rickrack braid, 1cm (⅜in) wide • Three pink heart buttons, 1cm (⅜in) high • 120cm (48in) of white satin ribbon, 1cm (⅜in) wide • Remnant of fusible web, such as Bondaweb • Refer to the patterns on page 85.

For each pennant cut two triangles. Decide how many hearts you want – we used three. Cut out the hearts and cut the rickrack braid into 3 equal lengths. Fuse the hearts on to the chosen triangles using the fusible web and stitch in place. Then sew on the buttons. Topstitch the rickrack braid in place.

Sew together each pair of triangles along both long edges, right sides together. Trim the seam allowances at the tip and turn the pennant out through the open top edge. Press the seams. Stitch together the top, open edge inside the seam allowance, so that nothing can slip out of place.

Fold the bias binding in half lengthways and press it. Pin the top edge of each pennant between the folded binding, placing the pennants 10cm (4in) apart and starting at the centre of the binding. Turn the ends of the bias binding inside and stitch the binding along the length, close to the edge, catching in the pennants. Finally, cut the ribbon into eight 15cm (6in) lengths and tie a piece between each pennant.

Lanterns

- 3 glass lantern holders — we used tulip-shaped jars, 6.5cm (2½ in) in diameter and 8cm (3in) high • Three 40cm (16in) lengths of red paper wire for hanging • Three tea lights • Strong adhesive, preferably hot glue • First glass: 45cm (18in) of twisted red satin cord; 25cm (10in) of narrow white cord and a wooden heart in white, pink and red, about 4 × 4.5cm (1½ × 1¾ in) • Second glass: 45cm (18in) of 4mm (⅜ in) red satin cord; 45cm (18in) of wired and beaded white ribbon and a wooden heart in white, pink and red, about 4 × 4.5cm (1½ × 1¾ in) • Third glass: an 85cm (33½ in) length of paper cord in pink, red and white; 25cm (10in) of white satin ribbon, 1cm (⅜ in) wide and a small wooden flower and butterfly in white and pink

Tie the long ribbons or cords around the top edge of the glass. Thread the red paper wire as a hanger around these ribbons to the right and left sides and secure in place. Attach the short ribbons and fix on the wooden motifs using hot glue and referring to the photograph as a guide.

23

For the Birds

Birdhouse

• 10mm (⅜in) plywood for the birdhouse • Off-cut of 3mm (⅛in) plywood for the hearts
• Wooden dowel, 10mm (⅜in) across and 8cm (3in) long for the perch • Durable acrylic paint in
red and white • Black florist's wire • Black permanent marker pen • White and red permanent gel
pens (or use paint and a fine brush for the markings) • Drill with 2mm and 10mm drill bits • Saw
• Wood glue • Refer to the pattern on page 86.

Cut the pieces for the bird box from the 10mm (⅜in) thick plywood: use the pattern on
page 86 for the front and back, cutting the hole from the front only (see the tip); for the
base, cut a piece 9 × 12cm (3½ × 4¾in); for the sides, cut two pieces 12 × 8.5cm
(4¾ × 3½in); and for the roof, cut one piece 13.5 × 12.5cm (5½ × 5in) and one piece
13.5 × 11.5cm (5½ × 4½in).

Transfer the heart pattern to the 3mm (⅛in) plywood and cut out. Drill a hole in the
front of the bird box for the perch and drill the hanging holes in the hearts.

Glue the sides of the birdhouse between the front and back and leave to dry thoroughly.
Glue both the roof pieces together, so that the larger one overlaps the smaller one
along the gable, then glue the roof to the walls so that it juts out evenly at the front and
back. Attach the base, which juts out slightly all round, and glue the perch into the little
hole in the front. Use screw clamps to hold the individual pieces while they dry. For
added strength, you can use panel pins to secure the pieces together.

Paint the birdhouse and the hearts using the pattern and photograph as your guide.
Draw the lines and decorations with the permanent marker pen and gel pens or using a
fine brush and paint. Attach the wire hangers to the hearts and tie to the perch.

Tip

An easy way to cut the hole for the birdhouse entrance is to use a 30mm (1¼in) core
drill bit. Alternatively, drill a small hole anywhere on the outline for the opening, slide a
jigsaw blade through the hole and then carefully cut around the outline. Use sandpaper
to smooth the hole afterwards.

Kitchen Comforts

Red and white are popular colours for kitchens and breakfast rooms because they make such a fresh and cheerful combination. After all, the practical things in life ought to look nice too. We have produced a number of projects here in red and white to brighten your day and create a nice atmosphere too. You will find an apron for an adult and child, tea towels, a chalk board, a bag and more.

The Smart Cook

Adult's apron

• 90cm (1yd) of pink-and-red floral fabric for the apron • Assortment of coordinating fabrics — we used 30cm (12in) of red fabric with white spots; 25cm (10in) of pink-and-white gingham fabric; 15cm (6in) of rose-patterned fabric and a remnant of pale pink cotton • Remnant of fusible web, such as Bondaweb • 2.3m (2½ yd) of ribbon to decorate the waistband tie • Black permanent fabric marker pen • Pinking shears • 3 braces clips • Refer to the diagram on page 86.

Getting started

Use the diagram on page 86 to cut the main apron shape (without the ties or pocket). Cut the top curves by folding the fabric in half lengthways, drawing the curve freehand and then cutting through both layers together. For the pocket cut 24 × 18cm (9½ × 7in) of gingham fabric, 14 × 11cm (5½ × 4¼in) of rose-patterned fabric, 10 × 4cm (4 × 1½in) of pale pink fabric and 18 × 6.5cm (7 × 2½in) of spotted fabric. For the tea-towel strap cut 9 × 7cm (3½ × 2¾in) of gingham fabric. For the waistband tie cut 230 × 7cm (90½ × 2¾in) of spotted fabric, joining lengths of fabric as necessary, and for the neck strap cut 60 × 8cm (23½ × 3¼in) of spotted fabric.

Turn a scant 1cm (⅜in) double hem all around the apron and topstitch close to the edge, starting with the sides, then the top and the bottom edges – you may need to snip the turning on the arm curves so it lies flat. Turn 1cm (⅜in) to the wrong side along both short edges of the pocket and turn a double 1.5cm (⅝in) hem along the top edge. Press the hems and topstitch close to the edge.

Appliquéd pocket

Iron 1cm (⅜in) to the wrong side all around the rose-patterned rectangle, rounding off the bottom corners for the marmalade jar shape. Pin this to the pocket, 2.5cm (1in) from the bottom raw edge and about 4.5cm (1¾in) from each side; topstitch close to the edge. For the label, cut out a 10 × 4cm (4 × 1½in) rectangle of fusible web and iron it on to the pale pink fabric. Cut it out using the pinking shears. Write the word 'Marmalade' on the label using the fabric marker pen and iron the label on to the rose fabric 2cm (¾in) below the top edge and 1cm (⅜in) away from each side (see the instructions on page 82).

Turn a double 1cm (⅜in) hem on the lower long edge of the smallest strip of spotted fabric and topstitch close to the edge. Press 1cm (⅜in) to the wrong side on the opposite edge and work a line of running stitch close to the edge. Pull up the thread to gather the fabric until it is 13cm (5in) long. Topstitch the gathered fabric to the pocket, positioning it 1cm (⅜in) above the marmalade jar. Remove the gathering thread.

Centre the pocket on the apron so that the lower (raw) edge is 1cm (⅜in) below the position of the waistband tie. Sew it in place along the sides and lower edge, stitching less than 1cm (⅜in) from the lower raw edge so that the stitches will be hidden by the waistband tie.

Instructions for making the tea towel are on page 35.

Making the ties

Press the strip of gingham fabric for the tea-towel strap in half lengthways, right sides together, and stitch following the width of the sewing-machine foot, leaving both short edges open. Turn the fabric out and press it flat with the seam centred. Thread on a clip and fold the strip in half so the seam is hidden.

Fold the waistband strip in half lengthways with right sides together and stitch following the width of the sewing-machine foot and leaving one short edge open. Now turn out the strip (a long knitting needle can be used to help with this). Press the waistband tie then turn in a narrow seam allowance at the open end and stitch closed by hand. Pin the waistband tie centred on the apron so that it covers the bottom of the pocket. Slip the tea-towel strap underneath it too, using the diagram as a guide. Topstitch the tie in place along the top and bottom edges, close to the edge of the fabric, catching in the pocket and tea-towel strap. Sew the ribbon centred on the waistband tape, turning in the ends to neaten them.

Finally, press the remaining fabric (for the neck strap) in half lengthways, right sides together, and sew together following the width of the sewing-machine foot, but leaving both short ends open. Turn out the strap, iron flat with the seam centred on the back and thread a clip on to each end. Turn the raw edges to the back twice by 1cm (⅜in) on each end, enclosing a clip, and topstitch close to the edge. Now the strap can be attached to the apron using the clips.

Child's apron

• 46 × 62cm (18 × 24 ½ in) of red fabric with white spots • 17 × 13cm (6¾ × 5in) of rose-patterned fabric for the pocket • 150 × 6cm (59 × 2 ½ in) and 54 × 5cm (21 ¼ × 2in) of pink-and-white gingham for the ties • 1.8m (70in) of white rickrack braid, 1cm (⅜in) wide • 30cm (12in) of red satin ribbon with white spots, 1.5cm (⅝in) wide • Refer to the diagram on page 86.

Shape the apron following the diagram on page 86 – the exact curve at the arms is not important, but both should be shaped the same. To cut the curves, fold the fabric in half lengthways then draw the curve freehand; cut out through both layers.

The apron, pocket and waistband tape are made as described for the adult's apron, but without the decoration on the pocket or the tea-towel clip. Fold the waistband tape in half lengthways and pin rickrack braid between the layers along the long edge so that when turned out, the braid will create a scalloped edging. Stitch one end and along the length using the width of your sewing foot as a guide. Finish the waistband as for the adult's apron.

Make the neck strap as described for the adult's apron, but without the clips. Sew both ends to the top corners of the apron on the wrong side and sew the remaining rickrack braid to the top edge of the apron on the right side, using the photograph as a guide. Tie the satin ribbon into a bow and sew by hand on to the centre of the pocket.

Breakfast Bonanza

Decorative wreath

- 25cm (10in) foam wreath • 11 × 300cm (4 ¼ × 118in) of red towelling fabric — two 150cm (59in) strips can be joined together to make up the length • 11 × 300cm (4 ¼ × 118in) of wadding — you can join lengths as required • Pink and red ribbon • Red cord, 4mm (³⁄₁₆in) in diameter • Selection of pink and red artificial flowers • Small pink artificial roses • Textile adhesive

Turn under one long edge of the towelling strip by 1cm (⅜in) and press in place. Wrap the wadding around the wreath, overlapping it as you go, and secure the end with adhesive. Now wind the towelling strip around the wreath, overlapping it so that the neatened edge covers the raw one and completely covering the wadding. Turn the end under and sew in place with a few hand stitches.

Wind the cord around the wreath, leaving 30cm (12in) at the start and end; tie in place. Thread two artificial flowers to the stems of the little roses and secure each stem to the cord, distributing the flowers evenly around the wreath. Wind the ribbon, like the cord, around the wreath and tie the ends into a bow. Now hang your wreath from a ribbon loop.

Tray

- 18 × 31cm (7 × 12 ¼ in) wooden tray • Acrylic paint in white and red • Découpage varnish • Vichy check pink paper napkin • Paper napkin with teapot design or other suitable motif • Sharp, pointed scissors

Paint the tray with two coats of white acrylic paint. Cut the checked paper napkin to the size of the tray base and apply it using the découpage technique (see page 82). When dry, cut out the teapot motif from the other napkin and fix it in the centre using the same technique. Paint the top edge of the tray with two coats of red acrylic paint, leave to dry and seal all the surfaces with découpage varnish.

Coaster

• 20cm (8in) round cork coaster • White acrylic paint
• Red paper napkin with white spots or other red-and-
white napkin • Découpage varnish • About 1m (40in)
of pink Vichy check ribbon to fit the depth of the coaster
• 1cm (⅜in) high heart-shaped button • Textile adhesive
• Refer to the bow diagram on page 85.

Paint the top and the edge of the coaster with
two coats of acrylic paint to seal it and leave to
dry. Place the coaster on to the wrong side of the
paper napkin, trace around the outline and cut
out the paper circle. Use the découpage
technique (see page 82) to apply the paper to
the top of the coaster.

Glue the ribbon around the edge of the coaster
and make a bow (see page 85). Decorate the
bow with the little heart button and glue over the
ends of the ribbon.

Cutlery holder

• 13cm (5in) cube-shaped wooden container • White
acrylic paint • Découpage varnish • Paper napkins with
teapot design or other suitable motif • 56cm (22in) of
red satin ribbon with white spots, 1.5cm (⅝in) wide
• Multi-purpose adhesive

Paint the wooden container inside and out with
two coats of acrylic paint and leave to dry. Cut
out two teapots from the paper napkins and use
the découpage technique (see page 82) to fix
them centred on two opposite sides.

Glue the satin ribbon around the top edge,
pulling the ribbon taut; turn under the end by
1cm (⅜in) to neaten it and trim any excess. Seal
all the surfaces with découpage varnish.

Tip
You can buy MDF blanks in the form of trays,
coasters, boxes, picture frames and more, which
are ideal for the projects in this section. Do not
worry if you cannot find the exact sizes used here
– just choose the nearest equivalent.

Tea towels

- 64 × 46cm (25 × 18in) rectangle of red towelling fabric, cut with one short edge on the selvedge • 46 × 13cm (18 × 5in) strip of pink-and-red cotton fabric • 1.3m (51in) of coordinating bias binding, 2cm (¾in) wide

Press 1cm (⅜in) to the wrong side along one long edge of the cotton fabric. Place the opposite long edge to the short raw edge of the towelling fabric with right sides facing and sew a 1cm (⅜in) wide seam. Turn right sides out, folding the cotton fabric down over the towelling. Press the seam. Topstitch the free, folded edge of the cotton fabric to the towelling, using pins to hold it in place.

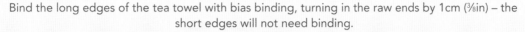

Bind the long edges of the tea towel with bias binding, turning in the raw ends by 1cm (⅜in) – the short edges will not need binding.

Tip

To make a hanging loop, cut an 8cm (3in) length of ribbon or tape, fold it in half and attach it to one corner of the tea towel. Stitch a decorative button with a rose or heart design on top as a finishing touch.

Chalkboard

• 23cm (9in) square wooden picture frame • 17cm (6¾in) square of 3mm (⅛in) plywood to fit behind the picture aperture • White acrylic paint • Red chalkboard paint • Découpage varnish • Paper napkin in pink Vichy check • Two artificial flowers in pink/red and a small pink artificial rose • 1m (1yd) of red satin ribbon, 1cm (⅜in) wide to hold the chalk and an off-cut of ribbon or braid for decoration • Pink chalk • Picture ring • Wood adhesive

Paint the plywood board with two or three coats of chalkboard paint. Paint the picture frame with two coats of white acrylic paint. Cut the paper napkin to the size of the picture frame and attach it using the découpage technique (see page 82), keeping the pattern lines straight. When it has dried, glue the plywood board into the frame using wood adhesive. Attach the picture ring to the centre back of the frame.

Place two flowers on top of one another and thread on to the stem of the little rose. Wind up the lower end of the flower stem into a flat spiral. Wind the ribbon off-cut around the inner flower and tie into a bow then glue the flower to the picture frame. Attach one end of the satin ribbon to the chalk and tie the other end firmly to the picture ring at the back of the frame, trimming it as required.

Tea caddy

• Metal tin • 7.5 × 5.5cm (3 × 2¼in) rectangle of floral fabric • 7.5 × 5.5cm (3 × 2¼in) rectangle of pale pink fabric plus a remnant for the wording • 7.5 × 5.5cm (3 × 2¼in) rectangle of lightweight wadding • Remnant of fusible web, such as Bondaweb • Pre-folded bias binding in spotted red or pink, 2cm (¾in) wide • Permanent black fabric marker • Two strong magnets

Iron the fusible web on to the wrong side of the pale pink fabric remnant. Write 'Tea' on it (or the name of whatever you wish to store in the tin) and then cut out, using pinking shears if desired. Fuse the label centrally on to the rose-patterned fabric, following the instructions on page 82.

Glue two magnets, centred 3cm (1¼in) apart, on to the wadding. Place the floral and pale-pink fabric rectangles wrong sides together, with edges matching and the wadding sandwiched in between. (The magnets should be lying on the pink fabric.) Pin to hold the layers together. Bind the edges of the layers together, making tiny pleats at the corners for ease. Now the label can be attached to the tin using the magnets.

Bag it, Box it

Summer shopping bag

- 50cm (½ yd) of fine red cord fabric with a floral pattern or other sturdy cotton fabric • 35cm (14in) of coordinating cotton fabric for the lining • 20 × 18cm (8 × 7in) rectangle of striped pink-and-white fabric for the front pocket • 30cm (12in) of red fabric with white spots for the trim • Remnant of coordinating gingham fabric • 70cm (28in) of fusible interfacing, 90cm (35in) wide • 30cm (12in) zip fastener • 10 × 17cm (4 × 6¾in) flower appliqué — make this yourself as for the cushion on page 18 or use a ready-made motif • 35cm (14in) of pink rickrack braid, 1cm (⅜in) wide • Refer to pattern sheet A.

Iron fusible interfacing to the wrong side of the lining fabric and the striped fabric for the patch pocket. From your main fabric cut two lower pieces, two strap loops, two zip facings, one 90 × 12cm (35½ × 4¾in) strip for the bag base/sides and two 140 × 12cm (55 × 4¾in) strips for the strap – each includes a 1cm (⅜in) seam allowance. Shape the ends of the strap pieces using the pattern on sheet A. From the gingham fabric cut two upper bag pieces. From your lining fabric cut two bag linings, two zip facings and one 90 × 12cm (35½ × 4¾in) strip for the base/sides. From the red spotted fabric cut four bag trims.

Turn in the seam allowance at the top edge of the front pocket and stitch in place. Fold the sides to the back along the dotted lines and topstitch close to the edge. Now press the fabric along the broken lines, matching this fold to the adjacent topstitched edge to make a pleat. Unfold and sew the pocket sides to one lower back piece (without catching in the pleats), following the markings on the pattern. Refold the pleats and stitch along the bottom edge about 6mm (¼in) above the bottom of the fabric, so that the pleats are held in place.

Referring to the pattern, make the four pleats on each lower bag piece, making sure that each fold points towards the centre. Sew each upper bag piece to a lower bag piece, right sides together. Topstitch rickrack braid to the upper edge of each lower bag piece.

Pair up the bag trims, placing them right sides together, and stitch along the wavy edge. Trim the seam allowances and snip into the curves for ease. Turn out the trims and press them. Now place a trim on each upper bag piece, matching the top edges, and stitch together along the top and down each side, keeping your stitches well within the seam allowances.

Sew the bag base/sides between the main bag pieces, right sides together. Repeat to attach the lining base/sides to the two lining pieces. For the strap loop, fold the long raw edges in to meet in the middle. Fold in half then sew the long side close to the edge. Sew the zip between the two zip facings and topstitch. Open the zip a little. Sew the zip facing into the bag opening, with right sides together, enclosing the ends of a strap loop at each end. Turn the bag out through the zip opening.

Iron the seam allowance underneath on each long edge of the two zip facings for the lining; these will be topstitched to the back of the zip. Stitch these facings to the bag lining along the raw edges, right sides together. Slip the lining into the outer bag. Secure the folded edges of the zip facing to the inside of the zip fastener with small hand stitches.

For the strap, sew together both pieces, right sides together, leaving an opening for turning of about 20cm (8in) on one long side and turn the strap out. Close the opening with mattress stitch and secure the strap by tying each end to one of the loops.

Drawer unit

- *Wooden drawer unit — we used one with drawer fronts that measure 11 × 7cm (4 ¼ × 2 ¾ in)* • *Acrylic paint in white, yellow, red and green* • *Black permanent marker pen* • *Refer to the patterns on page 87.*

Paint the drawer fronts white – this will make the colours of the paints brighter and clearer. When dry, transfer the patterns to the fronts of the drawers (with carbon paper or tracing paper). Colour in using acrylic paints as in the picture, using white wet-in-wet for effects and shading (see page 83). When the paint is dry, draw the outlines with the permanent marker pen.

Meanwhile, paint the box unit red with white shading.

Tip

Instead of the toadstools and gnomes you could trace off and use some of the heart motifs at the back of this book or paint all the drawers in stripes and spots.

Beautiful Things for the Home

We all dream of a stylish and comfortable home that we can be proud of. This does not necessarily require expensive makeovers — it is often the little things that make all the difference, which is why this section is full of stylish accessories, some with a festive feel, to help you create the look you desire.

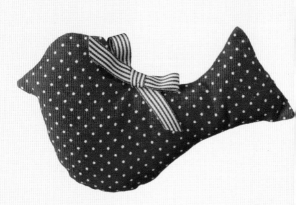

Room with
a View

Hanging cone

• 30cm (12in) square of red patterned card (reverse in spotted pink and white) • Scrap of red card with white spots • Scrap of pale pink card (or use the reverse side of leftover red patterned card) • 18.5cm (7 ¼ in) of pink ribbon with white spots, 1cm (⅜in) wide • 2.5cm (1in) heart punch • Hole punch • Thick red sewing thread or embroidery cotton • 50cm (½ yd) of red satin cord, 3mm (⅛in) in diameter • Strong multi-purpose adhesive • Refer to pattern sheet B.

Transfer the hanging cone pattern to the card and cut out. Punch out two hearts from the patterned card, two hearts from the spotted card and one pale pink heart. Twist the card to form a cone and glue along the adhesive tab. Cover the glued edge with the ribbon. Cut three 20cm (8in) lengths of red thread or embroidery cotton and knot them together at one end. Using a needle, thread the other ends from the inside through the tip of the hanging cone. Attach three hearts (two patterned and one spotted) to the threads as shown in the photograph.

Glue the pale pink heart to the front top edge of the cone and the remaining spotted heart to the inside of the back edge, as in the photograph. To hang the cone, punch a hole in the heart at the back of the cone and thread the satin cord through it. Knot the cord and glue it at the back or make a loop with the cord.

Tip

Use double-sided tape instead of glue to join the cone together – this forms a sturdy join and is less messy than glue.

Heart garland

• 15cm (6in) of red-and-white striped fabric • 15cm (6in) of red-on-red striped fabric • Two 62 × 5cm (24 ½ × 2in) strips of white cotton fabric • 15cm (6in) of fusible wadding • Two 1cm (⅜in) red buttons and two 1cm (⅜in) white buttons • Refer to the pattern on page 88.

Cut four large and four small hearts from each fabric. Cut four large and four small hearts from wadding and then trim off the seam allowance. Pair up the hearts and fuse a wadding heart to the centre of one of each pair. Now sew the heart pairs together, right sides facing, leaving the opening unstitched. Turn out through the gap and then close up the opening with mattress stitch.

Centre a small heart on each large, contrasting heart then place a button in the middle and attach the button through all layers using red thread. Sew together both strips of white fabric, right sides together, leaving one end open; turn out. Turn the seam allowance to the inside at the opening and stitch down. Attach the hearts to the tape, distributing them evenly.

Tip

To cut the wadding hearts accurately, trace off each heart pattern, mark the seam allowance on the pattern then trim this off. Now you have a pattern to cut the wadding.

A Touch
of Romanc

Flower girl

• 25cm (10in) square of white fleece fabric • 50 × 5cm (19 ½ × 2in) strip of pink cotton fabric for the frill
• Remnant of dark green craft felt • 70cm (27 ½ in) of pale pink satin ribbon, 4mm (³⁄₁₆in) wide • 20cm (8in)
threaded strand of 2mm rocaille beads • 25cm (10in) of white paper cord • Two wooden beads, 3cm (1 ¼ in) in
diameter and a 5mm (¼ in) wooden hemisphere for the nose • Two 4cm (1 ½ in) wooden marionette feet and two
1.8cm (¾in) wooden hands • Paper flowers with jewelled centres: two 3cm (1 ¼ in) in deep pink and one 4cm
(1 ½ in) in pale pink • Felt or foam flower in deep pink, 4mm (³⁄₁₆in) thick and 11cm (4 ¼ in) across • 9mm
(³⁄₈in) buttons for the rose bouquet: three pale pink and two deep pink • 4.5cm (1¾in) length of wooden dowel,
5mm (¼ in) thick • 2 wooden skewers • 16 strands of doll's hair in dark brown, 18cm (7in) long (bouclé yarn
would also work) • Five 14cm (5 ½ in) lengths of dark grey wire, 0.8mm thick • White acrylic paint • Black
fine permanent marker and red colouring pencil • Strong glue, preferably hot glue • Refer to the pattern pieces on
page 88. Seam allowances of 1cm (³⁄₈in) are included.

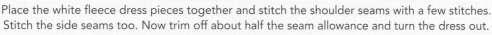

Using the patterns, cut two dress pieces from white fleece and five leaves from green felt. Paint
the wooden shoes with white acrylic paint and leave to dry.

Meanwhile, make five flowers for the bouquet. For each flower, bend a piece of wire in half and
thread both ends through a button from the front. Then place a felt leaf between both ends of
wire and twist the wires together so that the leaf is secured and the flower has a long, straight
stem. Tie the flowers together using the satin ribbon to form a bouquet.

Place the white fleece dress pieces together and stitch the shoulder seams with a few stitches.
Stitch the side seams too. Now trim off about half the seam allowance and turn the dress out.

For the pink frill at the hem of the dress, first join the ends of the pink strip of fabric into a
round, right sides together. Fold the fabric in half lengthways with wrong sides together. Work
running stitch along the long edges (working through both layers together) and gather up to fit
the bottom of the dress. Push the frill over the dress, right sides together, so that the raw edges
of the frill match the raw edge of the dress. Sew the edges together and fold the frill down.
Push the seam allowance up inside the dress and stitch down using small stitches, invisible from
the outside.

Now the flower girl can be assembled by gluing the pointed ends of both of the wooden skewers
into one hole in a wooden bead (body) about as far as the centre. Attach a wooden shoe to each
of the other ends of the sticks, ensuring that the shoes are nice and straight. This will give the
figure a firm base later.

For the head, glue the dowel (neck) roughly 2cm (¾in) into the other wooden bead. Attach the
little wooden hemisphere in the centre for the nose and then draw on the facial features using the
fine, permanent marker. Add a blush to her cheeks with the red pencil.

Now pull the dress over the body and the long legs and glue the neck about 1.5cm (⅝in) into the top of the body bead. Then, for the arms, thread the paper cord through the armholes of the dress and glue to the body bead behind the neck. Bend over the ends of the paper cord by 5mm (¼in) and attach the hands to them.

Glue the doll's hair across the head and tie the hair in bunches with the satin ribbon. Attach the paper flowers to the front of the dress. Wrap the threaded rocaille beads around the doll's neck as a necklace, glue the bouquet between the hands and glue the flower girl by the shoes to the large, deep pink felt/foam flower so that she stands firmly.

Tea-light hanging

- *Wired spherical tea-light holder, roughly 15cm (6in) across* • *Remnant of red-and-white gingham fabric and rose-pattern fabric* • *Small amount of wadding* • *2cm (¾in) white button* • *1cm (⅜in) red heart button* • *20cm (8in) of white wire* • *35cm (14in) of rose-patterned ribbon, 2cm (¾in) wide* • *Metal hearts in red and pink, 1cm (⅜in) high* • *Small amount of invisible thread or fishing line* • *Hot-glue gun and glue* • *Refer to the pattern on page 89. Seam allowances of 1cm (⅜in) are included.*

Cut each half heart in each fabric then flip the pattern to cut each half heart again from each fabric in mirror image. Sew together a heart in each fabric along the centre seam, right sides together (a mark on the pattern shows where the top of the seam ends). Then stitch both hearts together, right sides facing, as far as the opening for turning. Trim the seam allowance and turn the heart out. Fill with wadding and close the opening with mattress stitch.

Thread both buttons together on to the wire, twist the wire into spirals and attach to the fabric heart using hot glue. Tie the woven ribbon on to the top of the tea-light holder in a bow. Attach the metal hearts with hot glue and tie the fabric heart beneath the ball using invisible thread.

Tip
If you cannot find any white metal tea-light spheres, you can spray another colour with white metal spray paint.

Note
Never leave lit candles unattended.

Table Decorations

Vases

• 3 white vases (porcelain or ceramic), roughly 13 × 16cm (5 × 6 ½ in) high • Ceramic transfer foil, such as Color-Dekor in red • 1.5cm (⅝in) and 2.5cm (1in) heart punches • Three hole/circle punches in sizes up to 15mm (⅝in) in diameter • Tweezers • Kitchen paper

Punch out the circles and hearts from the ceramic transfer foil. Briefly place them in water. Slide the foil from the backing paper on to the crockery or, for very small motifs, pull it off with the help of tweezers and lay it on. Smooth the shapes using your fingers and a piece of kitchen paper to absorb the moisture.

Leave the motifs to dry for 24 hours at room temperature. Then harden off by placing the decorated pieces in a cold oven and setting it to 180°C with heat from above and below. After 30 minutes, switch off the oven and leave the crockery to cool down in the oven (see also the manufacturer's instructions). Your finished pieces can be hand washed.

Flower tablemat

• Two 50cm (20in) squares of white fabric with pink motifs • Small piece of coordinating cotton fabric, roughly 20cm (8in) square, for the flower centre • One 50cm (20in) square and one 20cm (8in) square of fusible web, such as Bondaweb • 50cm (20in) square of fusible interfacing • Red machine thread • Refer to pattern sheet A.

Iron fusible web on to the wrong side of one of the 50cm (20in) squares of fabric (see page 82) and iron interfacing on to the wrong side of the other piece. Iron fusible web on to the wrong side of the small fabric piece. Fuse the two large fabric squares together with right sides out.

Transfer the pattern for the flower on to one side of the fused fabric. Sew together all around along the line with a narrow zigzag stitch (as for appliqué) in red thread. Carefully trim off the excess fabric around the outside, making sure you do not cut the stitches. Cut out the circle for the centre of the flower from the small piece of fabric, iron it to the centre of the flower and stitch around the edge as before.

Table runner

- *White cotton fabric with pink stripes: one 80 × 45cm (31½ × 18in) rectangle and two 10 × 45cm (4 × 18in) strips* • *Two 30 × 45cm (12 × 18in) rectangles of white cotton fabric* • *Rickrack braid, 1cm (⅜in) wide: two 45cm (18in) and two 80cm (31½in) lengths in apple green and two 45cm (18in) lengths in deep pink* • *Two 45cm (18in) lengths of pink bias binding, 2cm (¾in) wide*

First stitch an 80cm (31½in) length of green rickrack braid on to the rectangle of striped fabric about 8cm (3in) away from each long edge. Pin a white rectangle of fabric on to each end of the striped fabric, matching the raw edges and with right sides together. Stitch these in place, taking a 1cm (⅜in) seam allowance. Stitch the deep pink rickrack braid just beside the seam on the white fabric.

Now stitch a strip of striped fabric to the white fabric on each end of the runner with right sides facing and raw edges matching taking a 1cm (⅜in) seam allowance. Stitch a 45cm (18in) length of green rickrack braid just beside the seam on the white fabric. Finish the ends of the table runner with the pink bias binding. Turn a 1cm (⅜in) hem along the long edges of the runner.

Fabulous fungi china

- *White tableware* • *Ceramic transfer foil, such as Color-Dekor in wine red* • *Porcelain-paint pens in black and apple green* • *Hole punch* • *Kitchen paper* • *Tweezers* • *Refer to the patterns on page 89.*

Trace the patterns for the toadstool caps, with the motifs reversed (mirror image) on to the ceramic transfer foil then use the hole punch to punch out the spots. Cut out the motifs. Briefly lay the foil in water. Slide the foil from the backing paper on to the china, or for very small motifs pull it off with the help of tweezers and lay it on. Smooth each motif using your fingers and a piece of kitchen paper to absorb the moisture. Add the lines for the stalks of the toadstools and the grass with the black and apple green porcelain-paint pens.

Leave the motifs to dry for 24 hours at room temperature and then harden off the foil by placing the decorated pieces in a cold oven and setting it to 180°C with heat from above and below. After 30 minutes, switch off the oven and leave the china to cool down in the oven (see also the manufacturer's instructions).

Cuddle Up

Sonia the sheep

• 25cm (10in) of white cotton fur fabric • 12cm (5in) of red-and-white striped fabric for the legs • 10cm (4in) of cream cotton fabric • 10cm (4in) of red spotted fabric for the shoes • Wadding • Dark brown embroidery cotton • Two 13mm (½ in) deep pink heart buttons • Long needle and strong thread • Refer to the pattern pieces on pages 90—91. Seam allowances of 1cm (⅜in) are included.

From fur fabric cut two heads (one of them mirrored), two bodies and two ears; from cream cotton cut two faces (one of them mirrored), four arms (two of them mirrored) and two ears; from striped fabric cut two legs on the fold, and from spotted fabric cut four shoes (two of them mirrored).

Sew each face to a head piece, right sides together. Sew both head/face pieces, right sides together, leaving the neck edge open. Stitch together each cotton ear to a fur ear, right sides together, around the curved seam. Stitch the arms together in pairs, right sides facing, as far as the opening for turning and then stitch the body, right sides together, leaving the bottom edge open. For the shoes, close up the front centre seam, right sides together. Then sew the shoes to the legs, right sides together. Sew all around the legs and shoes, leaving the top edge open for turning.

Turn all the pieces right sides out and fill with wadding. Stitch together the openings at the top of each leg within the seam allowance. Tuck in the seam allowances of the openings in the arms and stitch closed using mattress stitch. Turn up the seam allowance on the open end of the body, push the legs into the body from below and close the seam, catching in the legs at the same time. Turn in the seam allowance at the neck (on the head piece) and sew the head to the body using mattress stitch.

Now attach the arms to the body as follows to allow the arms to move. Using a long needle, first sew through the arm from the top inside edge to the outside and then back through the arm and the body. Sew through the second arm from inside to outside and then back again from the outside through the arm and the body. Pull the threads tightly, drawing the shoulders slightly together. Attach both of the buttons to the shoulders, covering the thread. Finally, stitch the ears to the head and then embroider the features on the face, using the photograph and head pattern as your guide.

Tip

Snip into the seam allowance at the inner top edge of the heels to help the fabric lie flat when you turn the pieces out.

By Candlelight

Woodland table piece

- 40cm (16in) round wicker tray, whitewashed
- 30cm (12in) high lantern glass • White decorative sand • Red cylindrical candle, about 14cm (5½in) high • White wax sheet • Two tea-light glasses • Tea-lights in the shape of toadstools • Decorative toadstools in various sizes • Ivy strands • Red ribbon with white spots, 2.5cm (1in) wide • White ribbon with red spots, 1.5cm (⅝in) wide • Piece of wire

Cut circles from the wax sheet, warm them in your hands and press them on to the candle using the photograph as a guide. Fill the lantern glass with decorative sand and place the candle inside.

❁

Thread the narrow ribbon around the wicker tray and secure the ends. Tie the wide ribbon into a bow, tie wire around the centre and attach it to the wicker tray as well. Now place the glass with the candle in the centre of the wicker tray and place strands of ivy around it for decoration. Distribute the tea-light glasses and the remaining decorations among the strands of ivy.

⟶◦◦◦⟵

Table lanterns

- Two lantern glasses • Two metal tea-light holders • Red-and-white glass lampwork beads • Rocaille beads in white and red • Two 10cm (4in) lengths of wire • Strips of white felt, 1cm wide (Adjust the length to the circumference of the glasses) • Two felt toadstools, about 5cm (2in) high • Hot-glue gun and glue

Bend one end of the wire into a little loop and thread on the glass beads, alternating them with the rocaille beads. Hang the wire from the spiral of the tea-light holder then hang the tea-light holder in the lantern glass. Place the felt strip around the glass near the bottom and attach it, together with a felt toadstool, using hot glue.

Wooden Embellishments

Welcome wreath

• 30cm (12in) white willow wreath • 40 × 15cm (16 × 6in) piece of 4mm (³⁄₁₆in) plywood and 15 × 26cm (6 × 10in) piece of 10mm (³⁄₈in) plywood • 50cm (½ yd) of red ribbon with white spots, 2.5cm (1in) wide • Acrylic paint in white and red • Black permanent marker pen and permanent gel pens in red and white • Invisible thread or fishing line • Drill and 2mm drill bit • Refer to the patterns on page 92.

Transfer the large heart on to the thicker wood and four small hearts on to the thinner wood. Then saw out all the pieces and sand the edges smooth. Paint the hearts with acrylic paint, using the pattern and photograph as a guide. When the paint is dry, draw on the lines and decorations using the pens.

❖

Tie the red spotted ribbon to the wreath as a hanger. Attach the large heart and one of the small hearts to the centre of the wreath using hot glue. Drill holes in the remaining hearts for hanging and attach them to the bottom of the wreath using invisible thread or fishing line.

Tip
If you cannot find a white wreath, spray one in another colour using white spray paint.

Flower lights

• Chain of 20 lights • 4mm (³⁄₁₆in) plywood sufficient to cut 20 flowers, each 10cm (4in) across • Acrylic paint in white and red • Glaze pens in white and red • Drill and 10mm drill bit • Hot-glue gun and glue • Refer to the pattern on page 92.

Trace 20 flowers on to the plywood and saw them out. Drill the holes in the centre of the flowers for the light holders and sand all the edges smooth.

❖

Paint ten of the flowers in white and ten in red, and draw on the decorations and patterns with the gel pens. Use hot glue to secure the small bulbs in the holes in the flowers.

Fabric Friend

Cloth doll and toadstool

• 30cm (12in) of cotton fabric in a skin tone • 20cm (8in) of red-and-white striped fabric • 25cm (10in) of white fabric with red spots • Remnant of grey or black fabric for the shoes • 15cm (6in) of red fleece • Remnant of red fabric with white spots for the toadstool cap and a remnant of white fleece for the toadstool stalk • Six 50cm (20in) lengths of doll's hair (or suitable yarn) • 40cm (16in) of red-and-white gingham ribbon, 6mm (1/4 in) wide • Two 13mm (1/2 in) wooden toadstool buttons • 1cm (3/8in) white metal bell • Black embroidery cotton • Wadding • Red coloured pencil • Long needle and strong thread • Refer to pattern sheet B. 1cm (3/8 in) seam allowances are included.

From skin-tone fabric cut two head/body pieces, four arms (two of them in mirror image) and two legs (cut on the fold); from striped fabric cut the cap (on the fold) and four trouser pieces (two of them in mirror image); from spotted fabric cut one shirt front, two shirt backs (one in mirror image) and two shirt sleeves (on the fold); from red fleece cut two waistcoat fronts (one in mirror image) and the waistcoat back (on the fold) and from grey fabric cut four shoes (two in mirror image). Cut the shirt neck facing as an additional piece. For the toadstool cut two stalks in white fleece and two caps in red spotted fabric.

Body

Pair up the arms, with right sides facing, and sew all round, leaving a gap for turning as indicated on the pattern. Turn the arms right sides out. Stitch together the two head/body pieces with right sides facing, leaving the straight bottom edge open. Turn the body right sides out. Pair up the shoes with right sides facing and stitch the centre-front seam. Sew the shoes to the legs, right sides together and raw edges matching. Sew the legs/shoes together all around, leaving the top edge open to turn through. Trim the seam allowance on the shoes and snip into it at the front corner for ease then turn the legs/shoes right sides out. Fill all the pieces with wadding.

Turn the seam allowance at the bottom of the body inside, push the legs into the body from below and close the seam, catching the legs in at the same time. Close the gap in each arm with mattress stitch and sew to the body as follows. Attach a strong thread to the inside of one arm. Using a long needle, first sew through the arm to the outside and then back through the arm and the body. Sew through the second arm from inside to outside and then back again from the outside through the arm and the body. Pull the threads tightly, drawing the shoulders slightly together.

Embroider on the face as in the picture. Secure the hair to the head in the centre with a few stitches and tie into plaits with the ribbon. Finally, draw on the cheeks with a red pencil.

Clothes

Turn in the seam allowance at the top and bottom of each trouser piece and stitch down. Pair up the trouser pieces with right sides facing and stitch the outside and inside leg seams. Turn out one trouser leg and push it into the other trouser leg, so that the inside-leg seams are lying on top of one another. Stitch around the curved seam (remaining seam). Turn the trousers out. Put the trousers on to the little doll and secure with a few stitches.

Sew the neck facing to the front edge of the neckline, right sides together, turn inside and topstitch close to the edge. Sew both back pieces to the front piece at the shoulders, right sides together. Turn the seam allowance at the neck edge of the back pieces inside and stitch down. Fit the sleeves into the armholes, right sides together and stitch the seams. Neaten the lower sleeve edges, turn the seam allowance inside and stitch down. Stitch the sleeve and side seams. Neaten the bottom seam of the shirt, turn the seam allowance inside and stitch down. Put the shirt on the doll, turn the seam allowance at the centre back seam inside and close the centre seam using mattress stitch.

Stitch the waistcoat fronts to the back at the shoulder and side seams with right sides facing. Attach the toadstool buttons.

Neaten the bottom edge of the cap, turn the seam allowance inside and stitch down. Fold the cap piece along the fold line with right sides together. Stitch the cap seam and turn the cap out. Attach the little bell to the cap and attach the cap to the head of the doll with a few stitches.

Toadstool

Sew a toadstool stalk to each cap with right sides together. Stitch both toadstool pieces together, with right sides facing, leaving a gap in the stalk to turn through. Turn the toadstool out and fill with wadding. Close the opening with mattress stitch.

Little Ideas, Great Results

Candlestick, picture frame and boxes

White candlestick — ours was 67.5cm (26 ½ in) high and 20cm (8in) wide at the base
• MDF picture frame with stand • 8cm (3in) white round cardboard box and 5 × 4cm
(2 × 1 ½ in) heart-shaped white cardboard box • Blue paper napkins with white spots
• Découpage varnish • White acrylic paint and clear gloss varnish • Ribbons in blue and red,
1cm (⅜in) wide • Red-and-white Vichy check ribbon, 5mm (¼ in) wide • Heart trim in
red-and-white gingham • Red satin ribbon and red rickrack braid, both 3mm (⅛in) wide
• Tiny red ribbon roses • 3mm (⅛in) red drop beads • Multi-purpose adhesive or hot-glue
gun and glue

Unless the candlestick already has a nice white finish, paint it with two coats of white paint and top with clear varnish. Sew the drop beads to the rickrack braid and glue around the candlestick. Glue the heart trim to the top edge and decorate with the tiny ribbon roses, having removed the green leaves. Cut four hearts from the trim and stick one in each corner of the base with a ribbon rose in the centre. Add ribbon trims using the photograph as a guide.

Paint the picture frame with two coats of white acrylic (front and back). Place the front face down on a paper napkin, draw around the inside and outside edges with a pencil and cut out. Attach the napkin to the front of the frame using the découpage technique (see page 82). When it has dried, varnish the front and back with découpage varnish.

Cut the heart trim to the width of the frame and glue to the top edge. Tie ribbon into a bow, attach a little rose (without leaves) to it and glue the bow to the centre of the heart trim. Glue Vichy check ribbon to the outside edge of the frame.

Place the round lid of the box face down on a paper napkin, trace the outline, cut out and attach to the lid using the découpage technique (see page 82). Glue the heart trim around the bottom edge of the box base.

Decorate the lid of the heart box with a heart from the heart trim and a little rose (without leaves). Glue red satin ribbon to the edge of the lid and tie the ends into a bow at the point of the heart. Glue the little heart box to the centre of the lid of the round box.

Instructions for making the little fabric bird are on page 66.

Fabric bird

- 15cm (6in) of red fabric with white spots • Wadding • 40cm (16in) of red-and-white striped ribbon, 1cm (⅜in) wide for the large bird only • 30cm (12in) of red-and-white cotton cord for each bird • Refer to the bird patterns on page 93.

Make a template of the large and/or medium-sized bird. Use the template to cut two birds the same size, flipping the pattern over to cut the second one in reverse. Knot each end of the cord and fold it in half.

Pin the fabric pieces together, right sides facing, placing the hanging loop between them at the top of the body. Remember that the main part of the cord will be between the layers so that it is on the right side when the bird is turned out. Sew around the bird, leaving about 5cm (2in) open for turning out the large bird or 2cm (¾in) for the small bird.

Snip into the seam allowance at curves and angles for ease then turn the bird right side out and press the seams. Fill the bird with wadding and sew up the opening by hand using mattress stitch. For the large bird, tie the ribbon into a bow, trim the ends and sew it on beneath the hanging loop.

Maidenhair-vine heart

- Strands of maidenhair vine (Muehlenbeckia)
- Brown florist's wire • Pink patterned ribbon, 1cm (⅜in) wide • 105cm (41½in) of red ribbon with white spots, 1.5cm (⅝in) wide
- Small red ribbon roses in two sizes • 6mm (¼in) pink pearlised beads • Textile adhesive

Shape the strands of maidenhair vine into a heart, winding them round and round with wire to hold them in place.

Tie the ribbon into little bows and glue the large roses in the centre, having removed the leaves. Stick on the decorated bows, the little roses (also without leaves) and the beads, evenly distributed over the vine heart.

Cut 55cm (21½in) of spotted ribbon and tie it to the heart as a hanger. Tie the remaining spotted ribbon to the hanger in a bow.

Garland

• 1m (40in) vase garland • 1m (40in) strand of artificial box or similar • 1.5m (60in) of striped red-and-white ribbon, 1cm (⅜in) wide • 1m (40in) of red-and-white cotton cord • Red and white artificial flowers • Heart trim in red-and-white gingham, 2.5cm (1in) wide — or cut your own hearts from fabric fused to fusible web • Textile adhesive • Refer to the medium-sized bird pattern on page 93.

Wind the box strand around the vase garland and tie the ends to the end fittings. Decorate every other vase with a small ribbon bow and place little artificial flowers in red and white in all the vases.

Cut the cord into five 20cm (8in) lengths and knot the ends. Make two medium-sized fabric birds as described on page 66 and tie to the garland with two of the cord lengths. Glue a heart cut from the heart trim to the end of each remaining cord and hang these to the garland too.

Candles

• Pillar candles in white, 15cm (6in) and 20cm (8in) high • Red wax sheet • Wax candle-decorating pens in red and white • Wax myrtle-leaf sprigs • Heart cutters, 4cm (1½in) and 2.5cm (1in) high • Craft scissors with wave blade • Artificial box garland • Striped red-and-white ribbon, 1cm (⅜in) wide

Candles with dots and flowers

Make the pattern of dots over the candles using the red wax pen and wind artificial box garland or ribbon around the base of the candle.

Candle with monogrammed leaf heart

Draw the heart on to the candle using a blunt pencil and carefully press the sprig of myrtle over the outline using your hand. Draw on the monogram using red wax pen. Using the wave scissors, cut a 1cm (⅜in) strip of red wax sheet, briefly warm it in your hands and press it on to the base of the candle. Cut off the excess with a kitchen knife. Make little balls from the wax sheet and attach above the strip, spaced evenly apart.

Candle with red spotted hearts

Cut out several hearts from the wax tablet using the small cutter and add dots using the white wax pen. Warm each heart in your hands before pressing it in place on the candle. Wind a short length of artificial box garland around the base of the candle.

Candle with red monogrammed heart

Cut a 4cm (1½in) heart from the wax sheet using the large heart cutter. Briefly warm the heart in your hand and press it on to the centre of the candle to stick it in place. Decorate the base of the candle with a sprig of wax leaves and little wax balls (made from the wax sheet). Draw on the monogram using the white wax pen and decorate the heart with a short sprig of wax leaves.

Instructions for making the fabric bird are given on page 66.

Gifts from the Heart

Little gifts are a pleasure to make and a joy to receive. From cards to containers and keepsakes, this section is full of ideas to show someone how much you care. We think that the combination of red and white is ideal for gifts and greetings cards because it emphasises the joy and happiness behind every gift.

Julia

With Love

Heart card

• 15cm (6in) square of thick white card • Coloured card or paper: white, pattern, light blue with white spots and red with pink spots • 1.5cm (⅝in) pink button • Remnant of white embroidery cotton • Two 14cm (5½in) lengths of white rickrack braid, 1cm (⅜in) wide • Adhesive mounts • Craft scissors with a scalloped blade • Black fineliner pen • Paper glue and glue pen • Refer to the pattern on page 95.

Cut out all the pieces according to the pattern, using the photograph to see which shape to cut from which paper. Cut a scalloped line on both light blue squares on two adjacent sides, along the cut-off corner of each patterned square and around the large white heart.

Glue the squares to the card and conceal the joins with rickrack braid. Glue the red heart on to the centre of the white heart and write the word 'love' all around it. Tie the embroidery cotton to the button and attach it to the heart. Attach the heart to the card following the pattern and using adhesive mounts.

'LOVE' card

• 10.5 × 15cm (4¼ × 6in) of thick cream-coloured card • Scraps of coloured card or paper: red with pink spots, textured deep pink and spotted pale yellow (for the oval), and other scraps for the letters • 30cm (12in) of turquoise rickrack braid, 1cm (⅜in) wide • Adhesive mounts • Four heart brads in red, 5mm (¼in) high • Fineliner pens in black, red and turquoise • Hole punch • Paper glue and glue pen • Refer to the pattern on page 94.

Cut out all the pieces according to the pattern, using the photograph to see which shape to cut from which paper. Stick the red oval to the card and draw on the decorations with the pens. Attach the letters to the pale yellow oval, following the pattern. Attach the rickrack braid to the reverse of the deep pink oval, so that the curves stick out over the edge.

Glue the light yellow oval on to the deep pink oval and use adhesive mounts to attach the complete oval to the card. Punch holes in the card using the hole punch and attach the heart brads.

Goose card

• 12 × 17cm (4¾ × 6¾in) rectangle of thick white card • Scraps of coloured card or paper: two light blue-and-red designs, pink, white, red and red-and-pink stripes • 2.5cm (1in) and 1.5cm (⅝in) heart punches • Black fineliner pen • Colouring pencils in yellow and red • Craft scissors with a deckle blade • Adhesive mounts • Refer to the pattern on page 91.

Cut a 7 × 13cm (2¾ × 5in) rectangle of light blue patterned card/paper and a 6 × 9.5cm (2½ × 3¾in) rectangle of pink card/paper. Trim the edges using the craft scissors. Cut a strip of the striped paper about 1cm (⅜in) wide and 17cm (6¾in) long and cut smaller strips from your second blue paper, using the design lines as your guide. Punch out one large red heart and three small pink hearts.

Now transfer the goose on to the white card using tracing paper and colour in using the colouring pens. Cut out the goose in a rectangle. Stick all the pieces on to the white card rectangle as shown in the photograph – the small hearts with adhesive mounts – and outline the motif with a broken line.

Gift tag

• Scrap of blue patterned card plus other scraps of card/paper for the decorations — we used red, pink-and-red stripes and spotted pink • 40cm (16in) of red-and-white cotton cord • 1.5cm (⅝in) heart punch • Craft scissors with a deckle blade • Hole punch • Refer to the pattern on page 91.

Cut out the gift tag and the individual pieces using the pattern and photograph as your guide. Punch a hole in the tag. Trim the edges for the nameplate with the craft scissors and punch out the red heart. Now put together all the pieces as shown in the photograph, write the name on the gift tag and pull the cord through the hole.

Tip

Use the outline pattern of the gift tag to make your own designs (see below).

Lotte

Treat Yourself

Shopping bag with case

• Foldaway shopping bag in deep pink • 20cm (8in) of red-and-white patterned cotton fabric • 10cm (4in) of red fabric with white spots • Remnant of pink cotton fabric with rose pattern • 23cm (9in) of fusible web, such as Bondaweb • Red rickrack braid, 3mm (⅛in) wide • 8cm (3in) of red satin ribbon with white spots, 1.5cm (⅝in) wide • Bag trigger hook and ring • Textile adhesive • 12mm (½in) press stud, with tool • Refer to the patterns on page 95 and sheet B.

Make a template of the bag case pattern from sheet B and cut the pattern from the patterned cotton fabric four times. Pair up the pieces, right sides together and sew the shaped top end between the marks, following the width of the sewing machine foot. Turn each pair right sides out and iron flat.

Fold the ribbon in half, wrong sides together, slide on the trigger hook ring and slip the ribbon ends between the bottom edges of the two case pieces, centring it at the mark on the pattern. Note that the main part of the ribbon should be between the case pieces with the raw edges matching the raw edges of the case. Stitch around the open edges of the case following the width of the sewing machine foot, neaten the edges then turn the case out and press it.

Transfer the small heart (page 95) on to fusible web, roughly cut it out and iron it on to the wrong side of the spotted fabric (see page 82). Cut out the heart neatly and iron it on to the centre of the bag case. Roughly cut the stabiliser to the size of the rose, iron on to the reverse side of the rose fabric, cut out the rose neatly and iron it centrally on the heart. Glue red rickrack braid around the edge of the heart. Attach the press stud following the manufacturer's instructions.

For the heart on the bag, draw the large and small hearts from sheet B on to fusible web and roughly cut them out. Iron the small heart on to the wrong side of the spotted fabric and the large heart on to the wrong side of the patterned fabric. Cut out both hearts neatly. Iron the large and then the small heart on to the bag. Apply a fabric rose as you did for the bag case. Glue rickrack braid around the edge of the large heart.

Bottle cover

- 64 × 32cm (25 × 12½ in) rectangle of red-and-white fabric • Remnant of red-and-white gingham
- 40cm (16in) of heart trim in red-and-white gingham, 2.5cm (1in) wide • 60cm (24in) of striped red-and-white ribbon, 1cm (⅜in) wide • 30cm (12in) of red rickrack braid, 3mm (⅛in) wide • 30cm (12in) of red-and-white cotton cord • Red ribbon rose • Small white gift tag • Remnant of fusible web, such as Bondaweb • Textile adhesive • Refer to the pattern on page 95.

Fold the rectangle of fabric in half lengthways, right sides together, and sew together across the lower short edge and along the side, taking a 1cm (⅜in) seam allowance. Iron the seam flat. Turn a neat double hem on the top edge, press and stitch by hand or machine – the stitching will be covered by the heart trim.

Sew the heart trim to the top of the bottle cover, so that the curves of the hearts overlap the fabric. Fuse stabiliser to the back of the gingham fabric and trace on the large heart from page 95. Cut out neatly then fuse the heart to the front of the cover, following the instructions on page 82. Glue rickrack braid around the edge and glue a small ribbon rose in the centre. Fold the ribbon in half to find the centre and place on the cover about 9cm (3½in) from the top, lining up the fold line in the ribbon with the seam in the cover. Stitch along the fold to secure the ribbon. Place the bottle in the cover and then tie the ribbon around the bag.

Write on the card tag and decorate it with a heart from the heart trim. Use the cotton cord to tie the tag to the ribbon knot.

Tea gift set

- White mug • Small white porcelain/china dish
- Tea infuser • Porcelain paint in red and white
- Polymer modelling clay in red and white, such as Fimo • 45cm (18in) of red-and-white Vichy check ribbon, 5mm (¼in) wide • 30cm (12in) of red-and-white cotton cord
- 34 × 22cm (13 ½ × 8 ¾in) rectangle of red fabric with white spots • Small white gift tag • 2cm (¾in) heart cutter

Subdivide the top edge of the mug into three equal sections and mark these with a pencil. For the curves, determine the centre of the curve and mark the depth 1.5cm (⅝in) below the top edge. Mark out the curves, hearts and spots on the mug in pencil, drawing on a large heart in the centre and two smaller hearts a–t the sides. Colour everything in using red porcelain paint and leave to dry. Draw the desired monogram on to the large heart in white. Decorate the small dish in the same way, marking two curves on each side 7mm (¼in) deep. Fix the paint in the oven, following the manufacturer's instructions.

Softly knead the red modelling clay and roll it out 5mm (¼in) thick. Punch out a heart using the cutter. Make a thin roll of white clay, shape it into a bow and place it on the heart. Make a hole in the heart, leave the heart to harden off in the oven in accordance with the manufacturer's instructions and attach to the tea infuser.

Fold and stitch the fabric as for the bottle cover on page 78, but without the appliqué and heart trim. Secure the ribbon to the seam on the back of the bag 3cm (1¼in) down from the top edge, stitching along the seam line. Slip a packet of tea into the bag and tie the ribbon around it. Write on the gift tag and tie it to the ribbon with the cord.

Heart box

- Cardboard heart box, 27 × 26 × 17cm (10 ½ × 10 ¼ × 6 ¾ in) • 20cm (8in) of ornate red-and-white cotton fabric • Strip of white fabric with a red pattern (for the white rose) • Red grosgrain ribbon with white spots, 2.5cm (1in) wide • White acrylic paint • Clear gloss varnish • Fusible web, such as Bondaweb • Textile adhesive

Paint two coats of acrylic paint on the inside and outside of the box lid, the inside of the box and in a border 3cm (1¼in) deep on the top outside edge (or to the depth of the box lid if different). Leave to dry then varnish well. Measure the box, deduct 3cm (1¼in) from the height and draw a rectangle to your measurements on fusible web. Fuse the web to the back of the ornate cotton fabric, following the instructions on page 82 then fuse on to the outside of the box, leaving the painted edge uncovered.

For the bow, measure the circumference of the lid, add 30cm (12in) for the bow, cut out and glue on flush with the top edge of the lid, starting near the tip of the heart and leaving 15cm (6in) free at each end for the bow. Make two red roses and a white one following the instructions on page 83 and glue these to the centre of the lid.

Coasters

• Wooden box with six square MDF coasters • White acrylic paint • Clear gloss varnish • Paper napkins in red with white spots and in blue-and-white and red-and-white check • Découpage varnish • Red satin ribbon, 3mm (⅛in) wide • Red rickrack braid, 3mm (⅛in) wide • Decorative foam bird, 3cm (1¼in) high • Textile adhesive • Pinking shears • Refer to the patterns on page 93.

Paint the wooden box and all the coasters with two coats of white acrylic paint and give the wooden box a finishing coat of clear varnish. Glue red ribbon around the top and bottom edges of the box. Add rickrack braid close to the lower edge too, using the photograph as a guide. Place the little bird decoratively in the front opening of the box.

Cut a 9cm (3½in) square of blue checked paper napkin for each coaster, using the pinking shears for a decorative edge. Attach to the centre of each coaster using découpage varnish (see page 82) and leave to dry. Using the patterns on page 93, cut two crowns, two birds and two mushroom caps from the red spotted napkins; cut the base of each crown, the toadstool stalks and the bird's tail from a red checked napkin. Fix a motif to the centre of each coaster using découpage varnish. When dry, coat all the coasters with découpage varnish. Glue the red ribbon to the outside edge of each coaster and tie the ends in a bow at one corner.

General instructions

Basic equipment

In addition to the items listed with each project, you will need a few basic tools and useful items including the following:

Pencil and eraser • metal ruler • all-purpose adhesive • hot-glue gun • tracing paper, dressmaker's tracing paper and thin card (for tracing patterns) • paper scissors and dressmaking scissors • rotary cutter and cutting mat • sewing machine • sewing thread (in a matching colour) • pins and sewing needles • iron • brush and water • fretsaw or jigsaw • drill with drill bits • sandpaper • screw clamps

Note: when the term 'remnant' is used, it refers to a piece that is at the most A5 size.

Transferring patterns

Depending on the material and the item, there are various ways of transferring patterns:

For paper and uneven surfaces, we recommend using tracing paper: simply trace the pattern on to tracing paper, hatch over the lines on the reverse with a soft pencil, then place the paper on the desired material and draw over the lines with a hard pencil.

Templates: these are helpful if you need to cut several pieces that are the same or when you will be cutting wood. Trace the motif on to tracing paper then roughly cut out and glue to thin card. Cut out the motif neatly, place the template on the desired material (e.g. fabric or paper) and then draw around it with a pencil.

It is best to transfer large patterns to the fabric using dressmaker's tracing paper. To do this, trace the pattern piece from the pattern sheet and cut out. Attach the pattern to the fabric with pins, where necessary, mark the seam allowance and any other marks then cut out.

Découpage technique

The découpage in this book is created using paper napkins. Motifs should always be traced on to the reverse side of the napkin. First separate the upper, printed layer of the napkin and tear or cut out the desired motif or pattern. Paint the background with découpage varnish, place the motif on the varnished area and paint it with more découpage varnish, so that it binds firmly to the background.

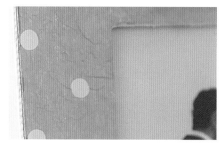

Tip
An easy way to 'cut out' a découpage motif is to draw around it with a small round artist's brush that has been dipped in clean water. The thin paper can be easily torn along the wet line.

Working with fusible web

Fusible webs such as Bondaweb are used to appliqué pieces of fabric or motifs. You can also buy interfacing that is fusible on both sides, such as Fast2Fuse, which gives a firmer finish.

Iron the web, paper side uppermost, to the back of the fabric. Then transfer the pattern to the paper backing, drawing it in mirror image because the right side of the fabric is the other side. Neatly cut out the piece along the lines. Remove the paper backing, place the piece backing side down in the desired position and fix it by ironing. To protect your iron, place a thin cotton cloth over the fabrics you are bonding.

Tip
You can use double-sided tape instead of fusible web to attach small fabric shapes to items that will not be laundered.

Fabric roses

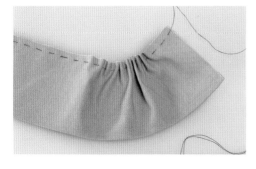

To make a decorative fabric rose, such as the ones used on the heart box on page 80, fold a strip of fabric in half lengthways, right sides out, and sew the open long edges together using a large running stitch. Pull up the thread to gather the fabric and roll it into a rose, turning the ends in at a 45-degree angle. Secure the end with a few stitches.

Sewing fabric

Use a sewing machine to stitch the seams of the items in this book or use small, neat backstitch. Close the openings left after turning pieces out with mattress stitch.

Mattress stitch

Place the pieces together (usually having turned the seam allowances under) and take a small stitch on one piece followed by a small stitch on the other piece. Continue to work in this way to the end.

Sewing corners

Fold the corner flat to form a triangle, then sew across the base of the triangle, cut back and neaten.

Note: the measurements given in the instructions always include the seam allowance. This is 1cm (3/8in) unless otherwise stated.

Sewing tips

• If you are making an item that may need to be laundered, such as an apron, wash the fabrics before cutting out the pieces in case of shrinkage.

• When using fusible interfacing, wadding or web, it is best to iron the product to the fabric before cutting out the pieces.

• 'Right sides together' means that the fabric pieces should be placed on top of one another with the nicer, front sides, or right sides, facing each other. 'Wrong sides together' means that the fabric pieces should be placed together with the back or less attractive sides of the fabric together. Some fabrics look the same on both sides.

• The arrows on the patterns show the direction of the fabric grain.

Sawing shapes

Make a template for each shape required (see above) and transfer it to the wood using a pencil. Then saw out the shape(s) using a jigsaw or fretsaw. Sand the edges with sandpaper. Drill any required holes using a drill and the specified drill bit.

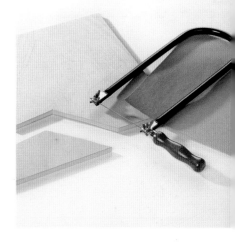

If internal areas have to be sawn out, start by drilling a hole on the edge of the shape, making sure it is large enough to take your saw blade. When using a fretsaw, remove the blade from the handle, slide it through the hole then fix it back on the handle. Carefully saw out the shape.

Wet-in-wet technique

This watercolour technique can be used with acrylics when shading is required. Apply different colours together or before the previous colours have dried so that where they meet they blend. The result is a flowing, soft colour transition. Always start with the lightest colour.

The Stylish Gardener

Watering can
Page 16

The Stylish Gardener

Gardener's apron and
kneeling pad
Pages 13–14

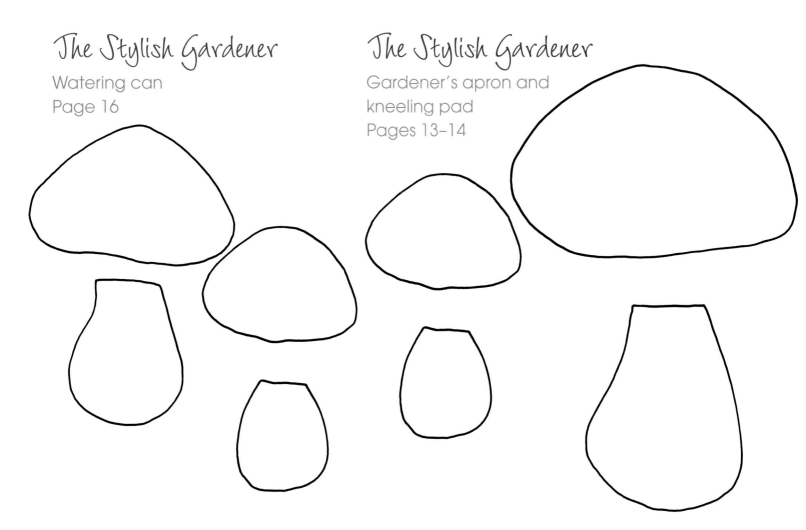

The Stylish Gardener

Herb markers
Page 17

Picnic with Panache

Patchwork tablecloth
Page 9

A	B	C	A	B	C	A
C	A	B	C	A	B	C
A	B	C	A	B	C	A
C	A	B	C	A	B	C

A = floral fabric
B = spotted fabric
C = gingham fabric

Lazy Days

Bunting
Page 22

opening

cut 2 for each pennant

Breakfast Bonanza

Coaster
Page 34

Bow

seam

stitch bow

fold bow

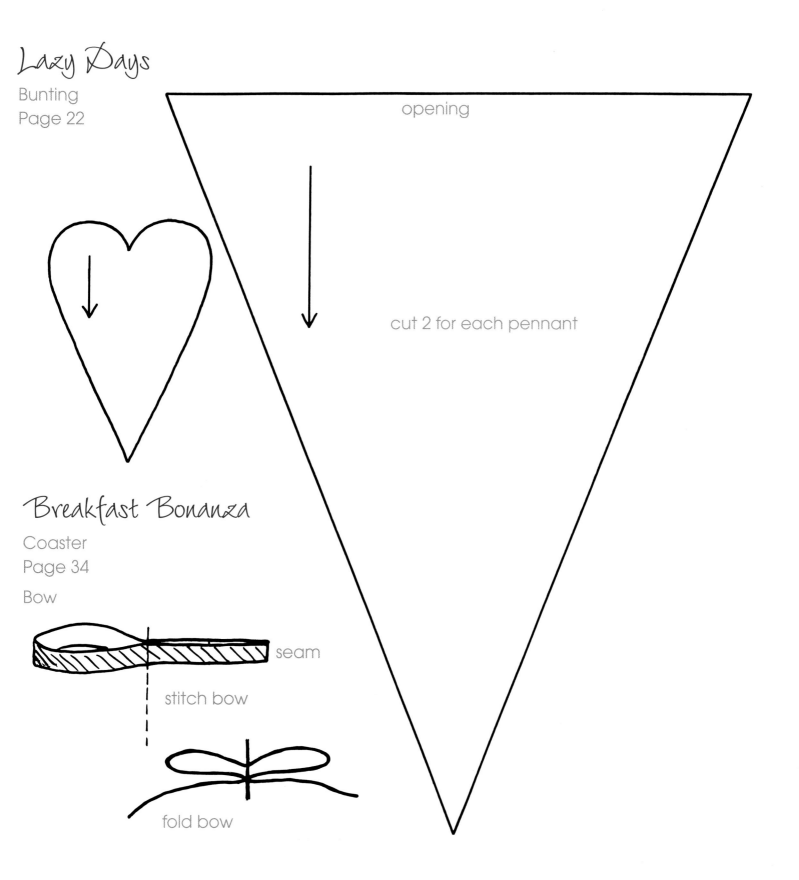

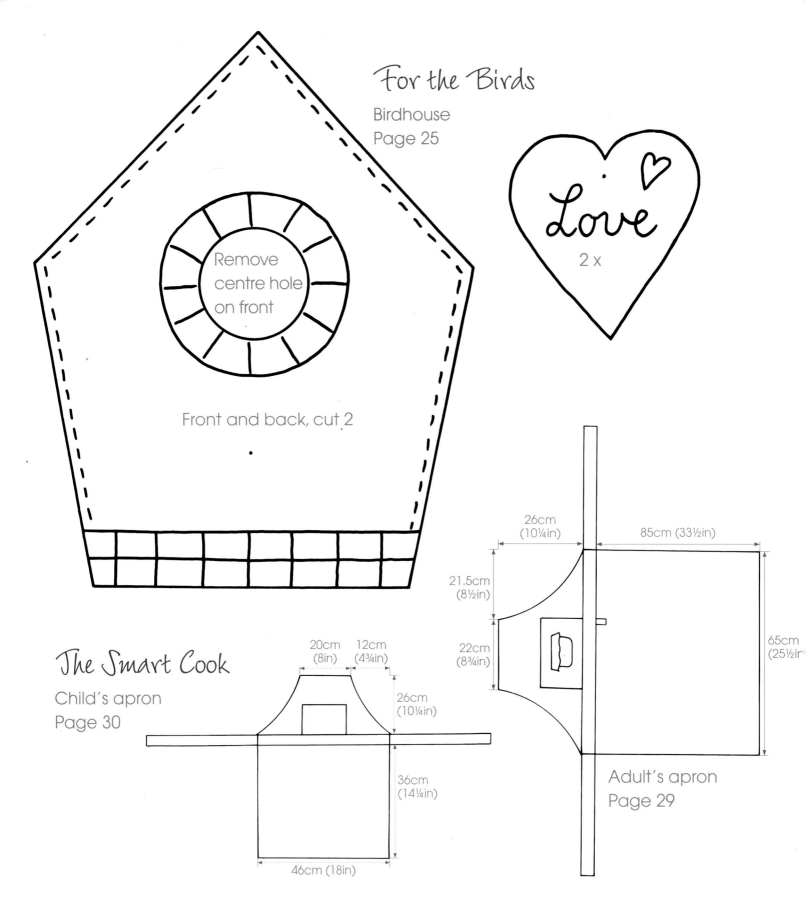

For the Birds

Birdhouse
Page 25

Remove centre hole on front

Front and back, cut 2

Love

2 x

The Smart Cook

Child's apron
Page 30

20cm (8in) 12cm (4¾in)

26cm (10¼in)

36cm (14¼in)

46cm (18in)

26cm (10¼in)

85cm (33½in)

21.5cm (8½in)

22cm (8¾in)

65cm (25½in)

Adult's apron
Page 29

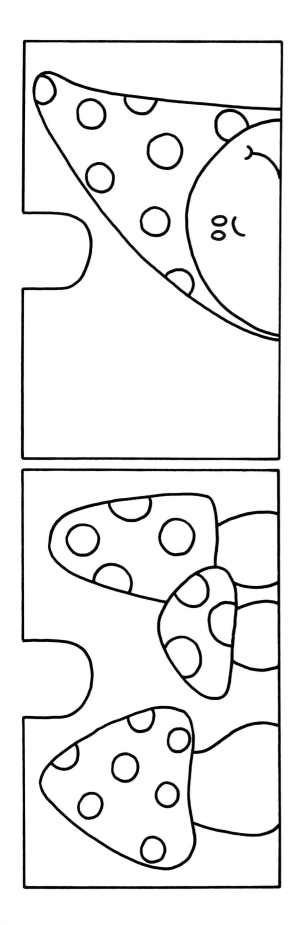

Bag it, Box it
Drawer unit
Page 41

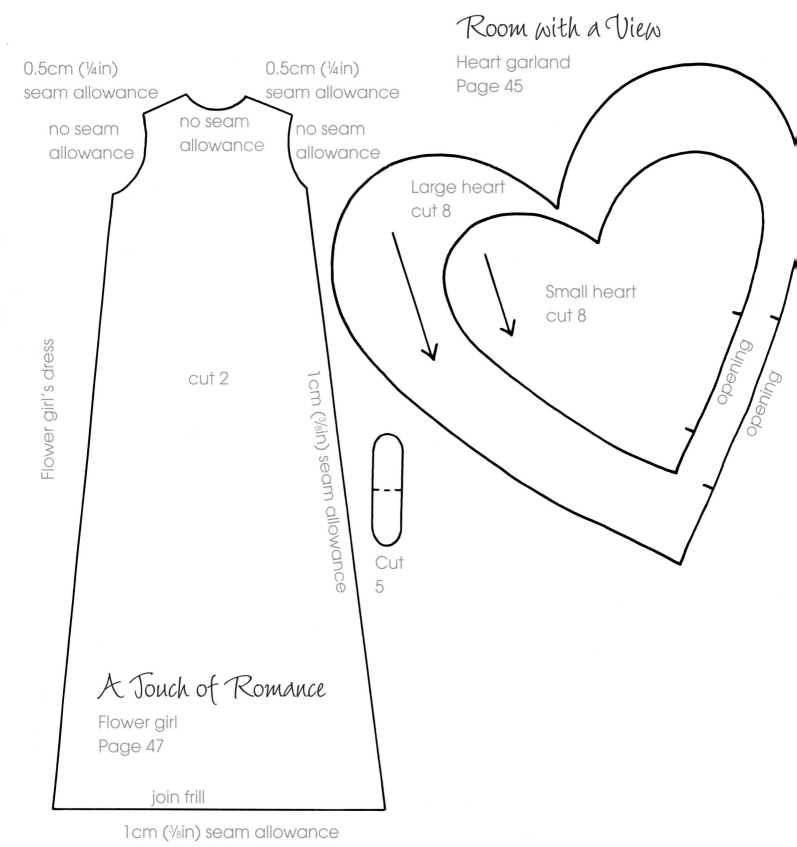

0.5cm (¼in)
seam allowance

0.5cm (¼in)
seam allowance

no seam
allowance

no seam
allowance

no seam
allowance

Room with a View

Heart garland
Page 45

Large heart
cut 8

Small heart
cut 8

opening

opening

Flower girl's dress

cut 2

1cm (⅜in) seam allowance

Cut
5

A Touch of Romance

Flower girl
Page 47

join frill

1cm (⅜in) seam allowance

A Touch of Romance

Tea-light hanging
Page 48

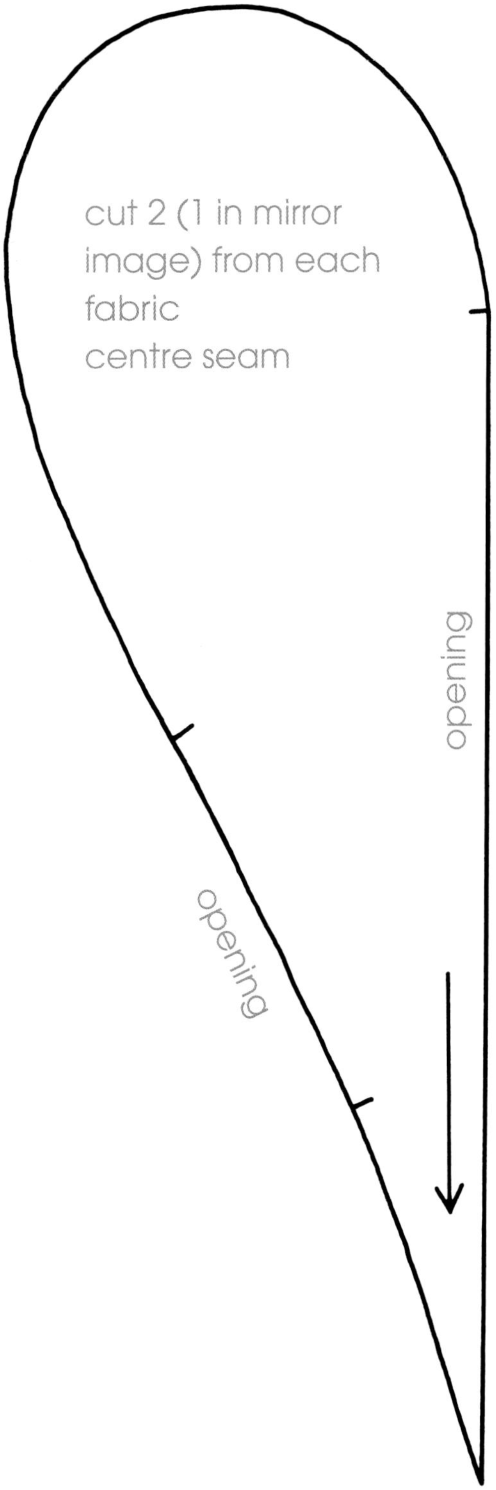

cut 2 (1 in mirror image) from each fabric

centre seam

opening

opening

Table Decorations

Fabulous fungi china
Page 53

Bowl

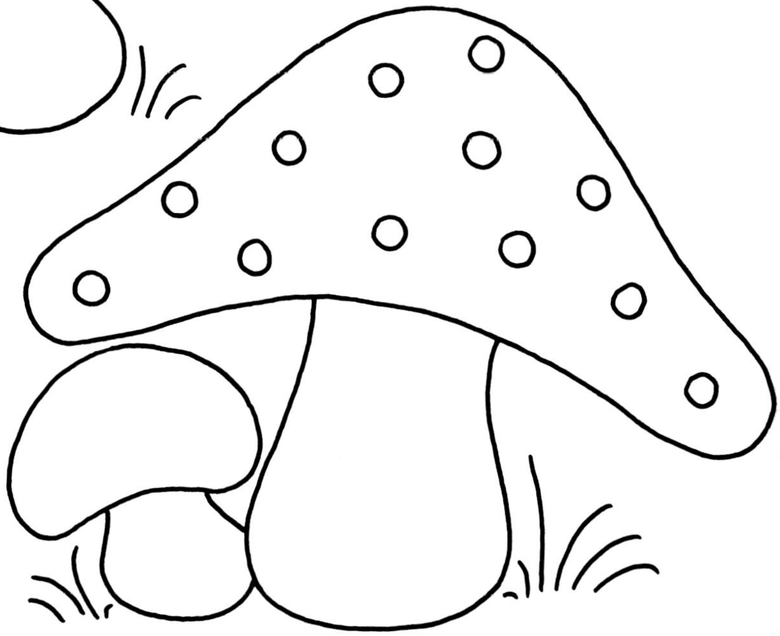

Mug and sugar bowl

Plate

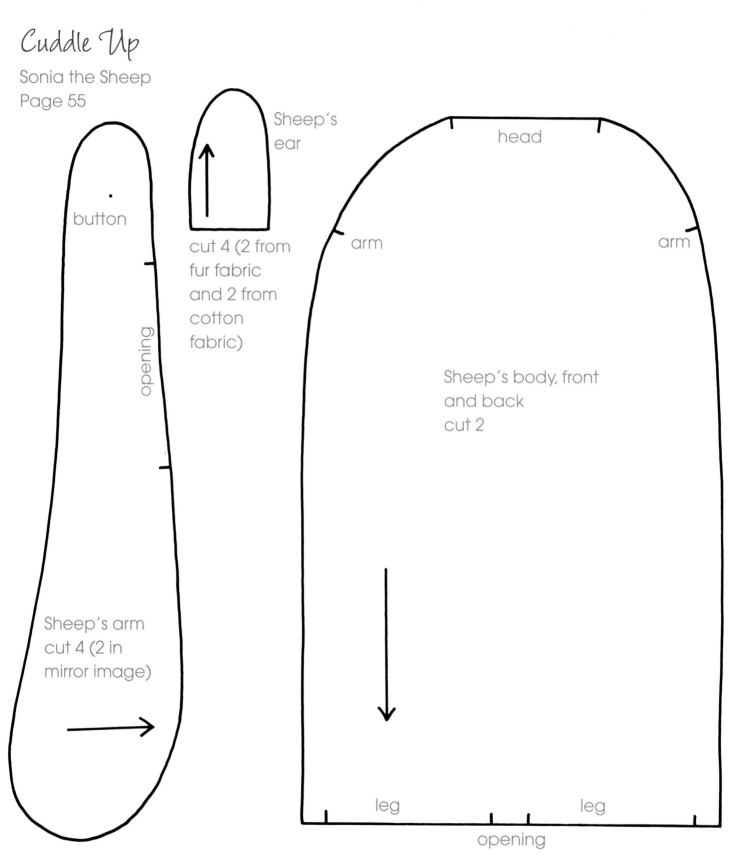

Cuddle Up

Sonia the Sheep
Page 55

button

opening

Sheep's arm
cut 4 (2 in
mirror image)

Sheep's ear

cut 4 (2 from
fur fabric
and 2 from
cotton
fabric)

head

arm

arm

Sheep's body, front
and back
cut 2

leg

leg

opening

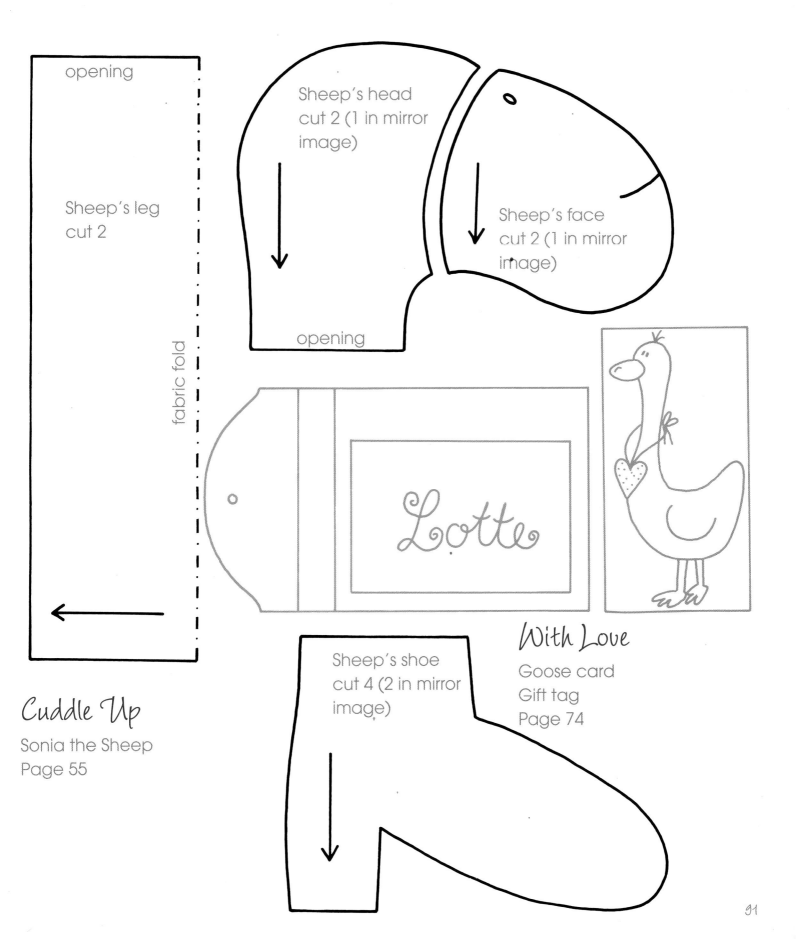

opening

Sheep's leg
cut 2

fabric fold

Sheep's head
cut 2 (1 in mirror
image)

Sheep's face
cut 2 (1 in mirror
image)

opening

Lotte

Sheep's shoe
cut 4 (2 in mirror
image)

With Love

Goose card
Gift tag
Page 74

Cuddle Up

Sonia the Sheep
Page 55

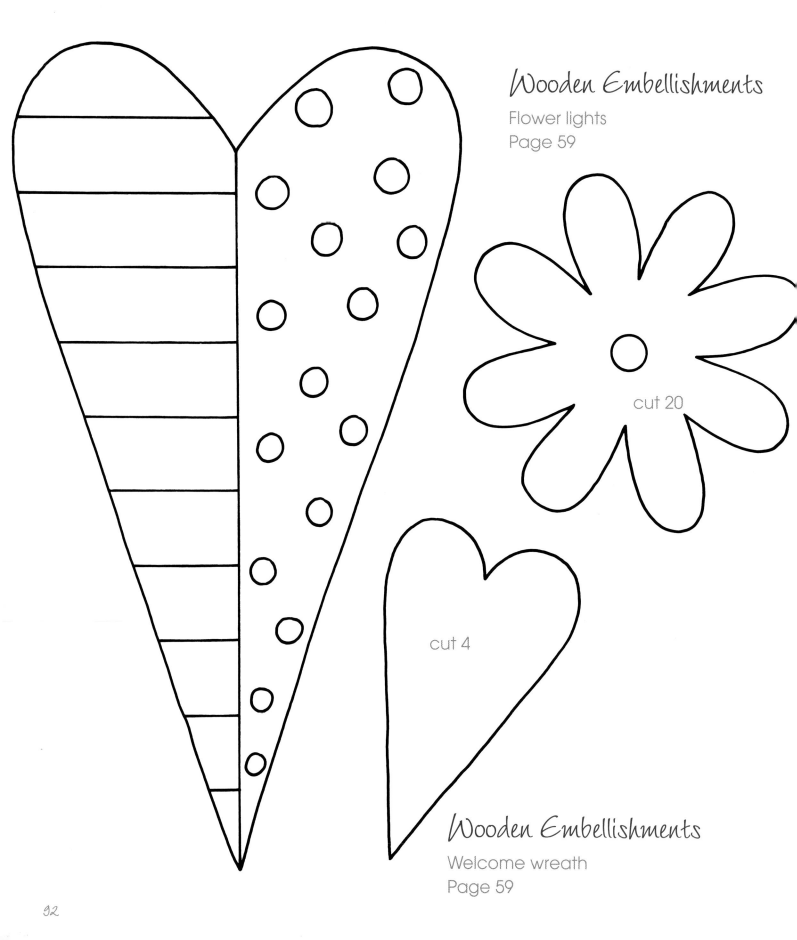

Wooden Embellishments
Flower lights
Page 59

cut 20

cut 4

Wooden Embellishments
Welcome wreath
Page 59

Little Ideas, Great Results

Fabric bird
Page 66

cut 2

Treat Yourself

Coasters
Page 81

cut 2

Little Ideas, Great Results

Garland
Page 69

With Love

'LOVE' card
Page 73

•2mm diameter

The Stylish Gardener

Gardener's apron
Page 13

Diagram for pocket piece

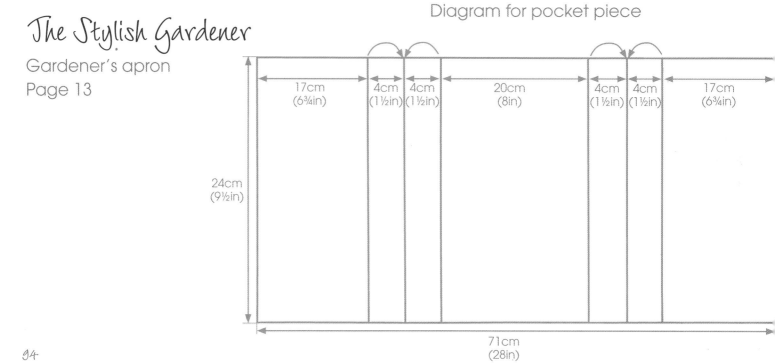

| 17cm (6¾in) | 4cm (1½in) | 4cm (1½in) | 20cm (8in) | 4cm (1½in) | 4cm (1½in) | 17cm (6¾in) |

24cm (9½in)

71cm (28in)

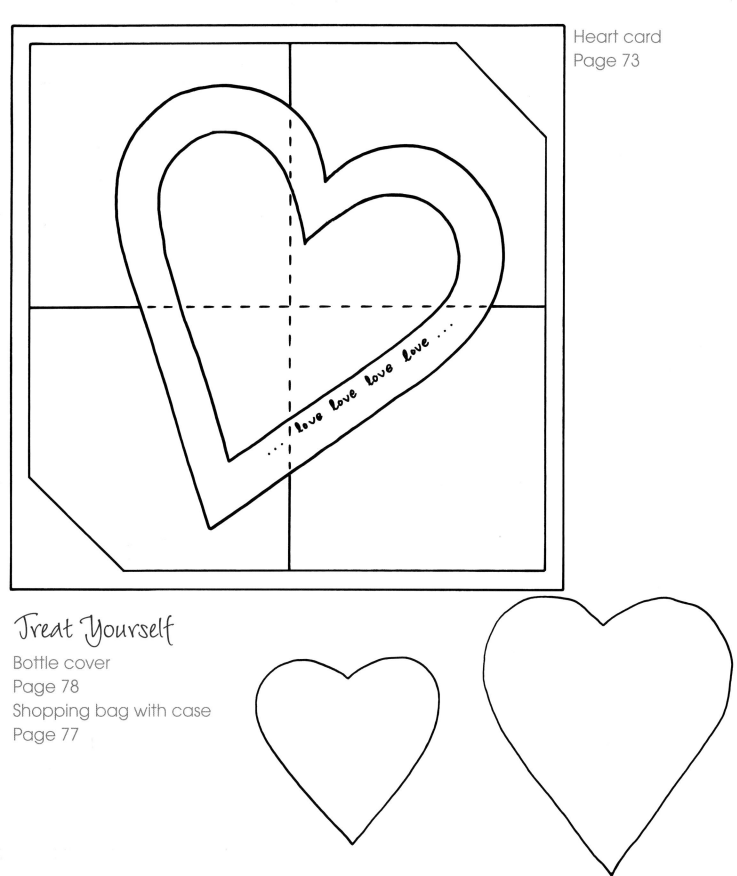

Heart card
Page 73

... Love Love Love Love ...

Treat Yourself

Bottle cover
Page 78
Shopping bag with case
Page 77

Publishing information

First published in Great Britain 2011 by Search Press Limited,
Wellwood, North Farm Road, Tunbridge Wells, Kent TN2 3DR

Original German edition published as Mittsommerland in Rot und Weiß

Copyright © 2010 frechverlag GmbH, Stuttgart, Germany (www.frech.de)

This edition published by arrangement with Claudia Böhme Rights & Literary Agency, Hannover, Germany (www.agency-boehme.com)

English translation by Cicero Translations

English edition edited and typeset by GreenGate Publishing Services

ISBN: 978-1-84448-748-6

We would like to thank the following companies: Gütermann creativ/KnorrPrandell (Gutach/Lichtenfels), Rayher Hobby GmbH (Laupheim), DECO-LINE, http://www.deco-line-kollnau.de (Kollnau), Veno (Bad Bentheim-Gildehaus), Freudenberg (Weinheim), IHR (Essen), Westfalenstoffe (Münster) for their kind support with materials.

ITEMS: Nadja Knab-Leers (pages 8–16, 28–37, 64–69, 76–81), Heike Roland/Stefanie Thomas (pages 17–25, 38–41, 44–63, 72–75)
PHOTOS: frechverlag GmbH, 70499 Stuttgart; lichtpunkt, Michael Ruder, Stuttgart